101 Games & Activities That Teach Leadership and Teamwork

Jared R. Knight

Disclaimer

Every effort was made to ensure that this book featured safe activities for participants, including a detailed list of the proper use of equipment and recommendations for the size of the group, age range, and safety precautions for each game. The author and publisher specifically disclaim any liability arising from the use of any information in this book.

ISBN: 978-1-60679-149-3
Library of Congress Control Number: 2010943135
Cover design: Brenden Murphy
Book layout: Studio J Art & Design
Front cover photo: Jared Knight
Author photo: Jenessa Taylor
Text photos: Jared Knight and Keeton Stewart

Healthy Learning
P.O. Box 1828
Monterey, CA 93942
www.healthylearning.com

Dedication

To my family: LaDonna, Rachel, Alex, and Emerson

Acknowledgments

I would like to thank my family and the editors and friends at Healthy Learning and the American Camp Association for their support and encouragement. Special thanks to the camp counselors and the campers at Aspen Grove Family Camp for their enthusiasm in playing these games during the summer in preparation for this book.

Foreword

As a longtime member and volunteer of local and regional Parent Teacher Associations (PTA®), I've found Jared Knight's writing well suited to assist in the accomplishment of the purpose of PTA organizations—in general terms, the character and citizenship development of children in partnership with educators and parents. His curriculum is adaptable in school classrooms and in larger school-sponsored activities. Each activity is simply understood, easily carried out, and highly engaging for participants in a way that helps them maintain interest while learning. This book *101 Games & Activities That Teach Leadership and Teamwork* will assist anyone looking to teach and even entertain young people in both meaningful and instructive ways.

Kenice Whitaker
President-Elect
Timpanogos Council
Utah Parent Teacher Association

Contents

Preface

I have been a facilitator for teambuilding games for over 20 years and in that time I have worked with hundreds of groups—corporations, public and private educational institutions, youth agency administrations, families conducting reunions, churches, and community leadership—but my biggest honor and challenge came this past October when I was asked to run a three-hour session for the president of Brigham Young University, his Leadership Council, consisting of the university's million-dollar donors, and their families. The camp that I work at, Aspen Grove Family Camp, is an alumni camp for BYU, and both the president and many of his donors have attended sessions there, so they were familiar with these teambuilding activities. I had a volunteer staff of 30 BYU students who each ran a game with over 300 people in attendance. The

event was held at the track and field area just south of the football stadium. Cosmo, the BYU mascot, was there interacting with each family. Many of the games included in this book were used at this event in efforts to build family fun and unity. In addition to the teambuilding games, each family made a family flag using fabric markers and a pre-made golf-type flag with a handheld flagpole. Each family also made up a family team name and cheer. By participating in the games, each family earned a BYU Teambuilding trading pin made especially for this event. (Other trading pins offered by the university include a BYU football pin and a BYU basketball pin that are distributed to loyal donors and fans.) I am grateful for the opportunity to have run this large-scale activity in preparation for writing this book because it gave me a chance to organize my thoughts and especially to organize the sections on processing questions that focus on the leadership principles learned during the games and activities and how to implement these principles in real everyday team situations. I have tailored this book to include age-appropriate teambuilding activities for both children and adults. I believe there is tremendous value in these teambuilding games where true leadership principles are taught and I am also grateful for the opportunities to not only write but to live these games and activities as part of my professional service to the university and to the camping community. I believe these games will benefit you in your own professional and volunteer pursuits as well.

Thank you,
Jared Knight

November 2010

Introduction

This book is written from the standpoint of the facilitator running each game and also asking the processing questions at the end of each activity. The facilitator's role is extremely important. He is the one that sets up the rules and the safety guidelines but then steps back and lets the team leaders and the members take on the important decisions. He is to help the team work together to reach the best possible choices by staying impartial and bringing out the natural leadership of team members. The facilitator is a sort of referee and he must not change the rules once the game has started. He should not limit creative thinking and thus steer the team with *his* opinions toward a specific conclusion. The best way of putting it is that the facilitator is the coach of the team, giving instructions and encouragement from the sideline but not taking the primary leadership role away from the team captain or other key team members. At the end of each game, the facilitator leads the discussion questions in an attempt to bring out the hidden leadership principle that the activity was built around. If the facilitator asks these questions in a natural way, team members will respond with meaningful answers. If the facilitator is routine about asking the questions, then team members will feel that they are being peppered with question after question and eventually respond to this interrogation with mechanical or pat answers. The facilitator should inspire team members and he brings out the best in the team. *101 Games & Activities That Teach Leadership and Teamwork* is full of wonderful games that are designed to help the facilitator do his job the very best he can.

1

Trust Games

Game #1: Caterpillar

Objective: To build trust in the decisions of the team leader

Goals of Participants: To complete a short walk while following a leader's direction

Overview: The team lines up single file with each person putting his hands on the shoulders of the person in front of him. The first person in line is the leader, and he leads the team on a 10- to 25-yard walk in a zigzag formation, creeping along like a giant caterpillar. The leader keeps his eyes open, but each person behind him closes his eyes and blindly follows the leader's direction and verbal cues.

Rules: Each person following the leader *must* keep his eyes closed from the start of the walk until the team reaches the end of the walk. If someone in the group is caught opening his eyes during the game, the facilitator can have the team start over from the beginning.

Preparation: The facilitator needs to set up starting and ending positions for the walk with cones.

Location: Outside on a trail or a playground area or inside in a large room such as a gym

Number of Participants: A team of 5 to 12 participants

Age Range: Five and older

Discussion Points: After the game, the facilitator should ask the leader of the team the following questions: What types of responsibilities did you have in leading the group? How did you feel having the complete trust of those that followed you? The other team members should be asked the following questions: How did you feel following the leader? What kind of direction would have helped you in your journey? Everyone in the group should be asked the following questions: When would it be appropriate to blindly follow someone? When would it not be appropriate? The facilitator could direct a question to anyone in the group that was caught with his eyes open about the consequences and accountability to the group for his own actions.

Safety Precautions: The team leader is responsible for communicating to the group when obstacles are on the course such as rocks, roots, or low tree branches so the blind followers do not stumble or get hurt.

Game #2: Conveyer Belt

Objective: To function as a team in order to establish trust in each team member as they attempt to cross a walkway made of boards

Goals of Participants: To travel one step at a time on boards held up by team members

Overview: A team of 15 people performs this task. All but one of the team's members line up facing each other (seven on each side, creating seven pairs). Each pair firmly holds a three-foot-long two-by-four two feet off the ground. The person that is remaining attempts to *crawl* on the boards. Once he crawls off a two-by-four, that pair moves to the front of the line so the line of boards acts as a conveyer belt and continues on until the person crawling on the boards advances 15 yards. When he has made it to the end, he steps off the "conveyer belt" safely and the group goes back to the starting line, where another person attempts the same challenge.

Rules: The person on the boards can only crawl and not walk on the boards. Two spotters should position themselves on either side of the members holding the boards to steady the person crawling on the boards as needed.

Preparation: The facilitator needs to set up a starting and finishing area with cones. Seven three-foot long two-by-fours are also needed for this activity.

Location: Outdoors on grass

Number of Participants: One team of 15 members

Age Range: 12 and older

Discussion Points: After the game, the facilitator should ask the following questions (looking for different perspectives from the participants crawling on the boards and the members holding the boards): How much trust was needed to achieve this task? How was that trust exercised during the game? The answers given by the two groups may or may not be the same.

Safety Precautions: Each person holding a board should hold it only two feet off the ground. He should kneel down on one knee, with the other knee upright to stabilize himself and prevent too much pressure on his arms or back during the activity. Team members with bad knees or backs should not hold the boards but should act as spotters during the game. The participants crawling on the boards should be either the same size or smaller than the team members holding the boards.

Game #3: Water Flow

Objective: To establish trust among team members while following verbal instructions and directions

Goals of Participants: To complete a task without getting a team member wet

Overview: One member of the team lies on the ground under a large tarp that the team is holding two feet off the ground. The tarp has six holes of various sizes cut out of it in different places. When the game starts, a half-gallon of water is poured on the tarp and the team tries to steer the water away from the holes to prevent the person under the tarp from getting wet. Team members can rotate positions so that everyone takes a turn under the tarp during the course of the game.

Rules: Because this game is built on the trust that the person underneath the tarp has in the rest of the team, great care should be taken by the team to prevent water from going into the holes.

Preparation: The facilitator needs a large tarp with six holes of various sizes cut out of it and a half-gallon of water in a bucket.

Location: Outdoors on grass

Number of Participants: A team of 5 to 15 members

Age Range: Six and older

Discussion Points: After the game, the facilitator should ask the following questions: While holding the tarp, how hard was it to maintain the trust of the person under the tarp? While lying under the tarp, how much trust did you really have in the team that was attempting to keep you dry?

Safety Precautions: The team members should be informed that they must stand in the same spot during the entire game to prevent anyone from stepping on the person under the tarp. The person under the tarp should keep his mouth closed during the game to prevent choking on any incoming water.

Game #4: Blindfolded Walk

Objective: To build the participant's trust in his ability to complete a task

Goals of Participants: To walk blindfolded through a course

Overview: Each participant, one at a time, walks a course blindfolded, attempting to make it back to the finish area without taking detours to dead ends.

Rules: Before starting, each participant is told that when he reaches the finish area, he will be greeted by the group leader. If the participant reaches an ending point and no one greets him, he knows he went the wrong way to a dead end and he needs to follow the twine back to the junction where he strayed off and follow another path.

Preparation: The facilitator should set up a course with twine or rope tied around fixed objects (e.g., trees, chairs, or cones) at waist-high level for all of the participants. The course should be at least 15 yards long with several outshoots leading to dead ends. However, like a maze, one line of the rope leads back to the finish area. The facilitator also needs blindfolds for each participant.

Location: Outdoors in an area free of tripping hazards such as rocks, roots, or tree branches

Number of Participants: A team of at least five participants

Age Range: Eight and older

Discussion Points: After the game, the facilitator should ask the following questions: What type of instincts led you safely back to the finish area? What were your fears or concerns as you attempted to complete the course? What would be some examples of "dead ends" in life that you should avoid? How can you make decisions with confidence that will lead to good choices in other areas of your life such as school, work, or church?

Safety Precautions: At each junction that leads to a dead end, a facilitator should quietly stand ready to assist a distressed participant. Other facilitators should stand behind the dead ends to prevent participants from wandering off.

Game #5: Flash Flood

Objective: To establish trust in the ability of team members to make good decisions on behalf of the team in a simulated emergency

Goals of Participants: To work as a team in transporting everyone across a makeshift bridge

Overview: The team attempts to cross a mock flash-flood area by using only six cinder blocks to form a bridge. The blocks serve as stepping-stones to form a line from one section of the playing area to another section, which is about 25 feet away.

Rules: As each block is placed on the ground where the "flood area" is, a team member must keep either a hand or a leg in contact with the block in order for it to be used for the bridge. If a block is set on the ground and a team member's hand or leg is not touching it, the facilitator can take the block away and the group has to cross the flood area with one fewer block. The facilitator can explain that the strong current swept the block away because no one was holding on to it.

Preparation: The facilitator needs six cinder blocks.

Location: Outdoors on a level playing area such as a paved or dirt path

Number of Participants: A team of 10 to 15 players

Age Range: 12 and older

Discussion Points: After the game, the facilitator should ask the following questions: Was this game taken more seriously because it was a mock disaster? How did you feel about knowing that your actions affected other people? If a block was taken away by the facilitator, was there blame or resentment toward the person responsible for losing part of the bridge?

Safety Precautions: A few of the participants should be able to physically lift the blocks a couple feet off the ground. The other participants that are going to be crossing the bridge should stand on the pretend bank of the flood area to prevent them from getting injured when the blocks are placed on the ground. The facilitator and other leaders should serve as spotters while the participants are standing on the blocks to help them if needed with their balance.

Game #6: Pole Crossing

Objective: To increase trust in team members by accomplishing a task that can only be achieved through the physical help of others

Goals of Participants: To crawl across a pole lengthwise without touching the ground, which is imaginary hot lava

Overview: A six-foot-long pole is firmly and horizontally anchored two feet off the ground by placing it on a cinder block at each end and having two people sit on top of the pole on both ends. One by one, team members straddle the pole in an attempt to cross it without touching the "hot lava," while the other team members assist the person on the pole by either supporting his legs or grabbing his hands to stabilize and support him.

Rules: The "hot lava" area is sectioned off by a rope on the ground that circles the area around the pole about eight feet in diameter. Team members cannot enter the sectioned-off area when helping the person cross the pole.

Preparation: The facilitator needs a six-foot-long pole that is secured to the ground, a large rope, and two cinder blocks.

Location: Outdoors

Number of Participants: A team of 5 to 15 participants

Age Range: Six and older

Discussion Points: After the game, the facilitator should ask the following question: In what ways did you exhibit trust in other team members?

Safety Precautions: The pole should be sanded prior to this activity to prevent participants from getting slivers. Participants should not exceed 180 pounds.

Game #7: Wagon Wheel

Objective: To establish team trust and unity in performing a task together

Goals of Participants: To function as a unit when moving from one area to another

Overview: A team of eight people form a circle with their backs toward each other and their elbows interlocked. The team acts like a wheel and moves, rotating clockwise, while walking 25 feet toward a finish line. One person is the team leader and yells out commands to the other members to take small steps in the proper direction.

Rules: The team communicates with each other while moving slowly so that everyone works together simultaneously. This communication should prevent anyone from tripping, becoming stretched out by adjoining team members, or becoming unattached from the group. Team members should be aligned with other members of the same height.

Preparation: The facilitator assists the team in forming a circle and in selecting a team leader. The facilitator needs cones to designate a starting area and a finish line.

Location: Outdoors in a flat, level area free of tripping hazards such as rocks or roots

Number of Participants: A team of eight participants

Age Range: 12 and older

Discussion Points: After the game, the facilitator should ask the following questions: (To the team members) How did you trust the team leader to follow his directions? (To the team leader) How did you trust in the other team members to execute your verbal commands?

Safety Precautions: The facilitator should watch for any member of the team to become uncomfortable, dizzy, or distressed during the rotations and, if needed, stop the activity immediately and reposition that person in the team or slow down the rotations before beginning again.

Game #8: Log Walk

Objective: To build trust in team members by practicing give-and-take in a teambuilding situation

Goals of Participants: To work with team members in order to stay balanced on a log

Overview: On a stable log that is laying on the ground, 10 participants line up facing the same direction, with half of the group crouching down and the other half standing up. The people that are standing up need to cross the entire length of the log by stepping over the participants that are crouching, without stepping off the log or knocking any of the crouching participants off the log. When the group has crossed the length of the log, they trade places with the crouching participants who then cross back over the log going the other direction.

Rules: If anyone on the team falls off the log, the whole team needs to start over.

Preparation: A large 20-foot log or telephone pole is needed.

Location: Outdoors on a flat, level area

Number of Participants: A team of up to 10 people

Age Range: Eight and older

Discussion Points: After the game, the facilitator should ask the following questions: As you were crossing the log, did you feel secure and supported by the team members that were crouching? As you were crouching, how much trust and confidence did you have toward the people crossing over you?

Safety Precautions: The facilitator should have five spotters to assist the participants on the log and to help anyone who falls off the log to land on their feet.

Game #9: Stretch

Objective: To reach beyond personal limits to obtain a goal through the help of and trust in other people

Goals of Participants: To reach an object that is just out of reach

Overview: A rubber chicken is placed on the ground about six to seven feet from a rope, which is the starting line. One at a time, each participant stands at the starting line and tries to reach the rubber chicken with the help of the other team members. The participant reaching for the object must keep his feet behind the starting line. Team members can stand on the other side of the starting line, but they cannot touch the rubber chicken. They can hold, support, and stabilize the participant in his attempt to reach the object.

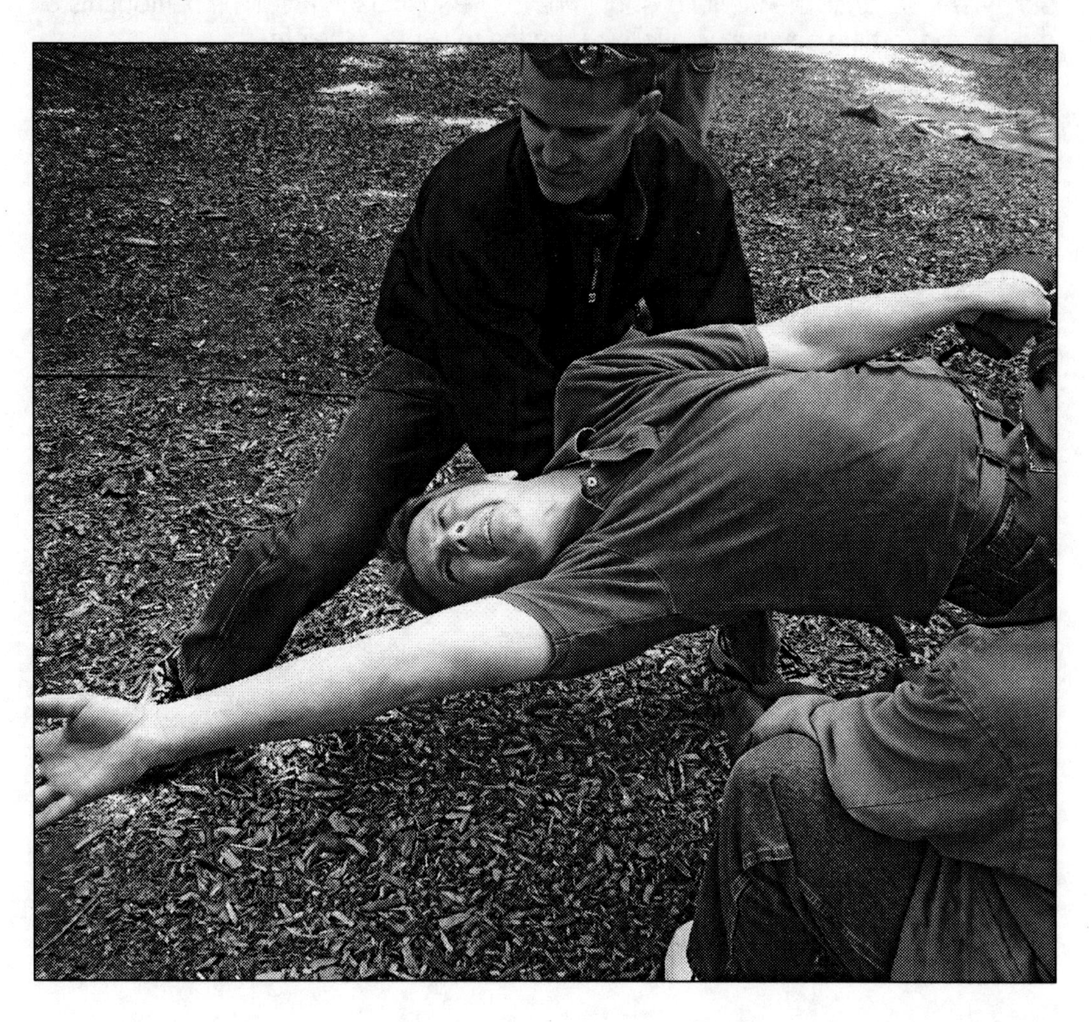

Rules: The participant can either face the ground or reach backward toward the rubber chicken. He can hold onto other people, but he cannot use anything such as a stick, rope, or article of clothing to bring the chicken toward him.

Preparation: The facilitator needs a rubber chicken, a tape measure, and a rope for the starting line.

Location: Indoors or outdoors

Number of Participants: A team of 5 to 15 people

Age Range: 12 and older

Discussion Points: After the game, the facilitator should ask the following questions: When reaching for the object, how were you able to achieve the goal with the help of team members? When helping the participant reach the object, what types of adjustments were made during the activity in order to achieve the goal?

Safety Precautions: To avoid muscle strain and pressure, each participant should stretch his legs, back, and arm muscles prior to this activity. The person reaching for the object should be in good physical condition and should not be lifted more than two feet off the ground by the other team members.

Game #10: Spider's Web

Objective: To increase reliance and trust in other team members as each member needs the collective help of the entire team in order to accomplish the task

Goals of Participants: To pass through a small opening without touching the sides by accepting the help of other team members

Overview: A large seven-by-seven-foot web made of rope is attached to trees, a freestanding wooden frame, or a freestanding PVC pipe frame, and participants attempt to pass through a hole in the web to the other side. The holes are different sizes to allow members of different sizes to participate. A stronger participant needs to go first so he can assist people through the web to the other side. When a team member attempts to pass through a hole on the top of the web, he should be lifted up through the hole by team members on one side of the web and passed through to members on the other side that receive him and carefully lower him to the ground.

Rules: Each time someone goes through a hole, that hole cannot be used by another participant. If a participant touches the web, he has to start the process again. A large, imaginary spider is approaching the web, so team members should work quickly but safely to get every member of the team to the other side as rapidly as they can.

Preparation: The facilitator needs a large seven-by-seven-foot web made of rope to attach to trees, a freestanding wooden frame, or a freestanding PVC pipe frame.

Location: Outdoors

Number of Participants: 10 to 15 participants

Age Range: Eight and older

Discussion Points: After the game, the facilitator should ask the following questions: How did you feel as you were being assisted through the web? When you were passing someone through the web, did you feel accountable to that person to ensure that he was safe and comfortable? What measures did you personally take to make this happen?

Safety Precautions: Communication between the two groups is critical as the first group hands over the participant to the second group. Once the person has passed through the web, the second group should lower him gently to the ground.

Game #11: Around the Tree

Objective: To find direction through the help of another person

Goals of Participants: To navigate around a tree blindfolded with the help of a team member

Overview: The team is divided into two groups and then members from each group are paired up. One person in each pair is blindfolded and the other person is the coach who navigates the blindfolded person around a large tree and then to the finish line five feet away. While the person is going around the tree, he cannot touch the tree for support. Both the blindfolded person and his coach stand at a starting line 15 feet away from the tree. The blindfolded person walks carefully under the direction and verbal instructions of his coach to safely approach the tree and then walk around it.

Rules: Each pair chooses a different tree at least 10 feet away from the other groups. All blindfolded participants are traveling the same direction so as to not collide with each other. After completing the task, the blindfolded participant and his coach trade places and perform the same task again.

Preparation: The facilitator needs a blindfold for each pair and cones for the starting and finish lines.

Location: Outdoors

Number of Participants: A team of at least 10 people

Age Range: Eight and older

Discussion Points: After the game, the facilitator should ask the following questions: As the blindfolded participant, how much trust did you have in the directions being given by the coach? What examples in life are similar to this game?

Safety Precautions: The coach should walk alongside the blindfolded participant and if the participant gets really close to the tree, he should stand between the participant and the tree to prevent him from hitting the tree. The coach is also responsible for verbally identifying hazards associated with the tree such as roots or low hanging branches so the blindfolded participant can avoid such hazards.

Game #12: Trust Fall

Objective: To conclude a teambuilding session with an act of ultimate trust

Goals of Participants: To fall back into the arms of team members

Overview: One participant stands on the ground and falls back into the arms of three other people. Two of the people that are catching the falling participant are on either side of him, supporting his middle back and arms, and one person is at the end, supporting his shoulders, head, and neck area. The person on the end should watch carefully to avoid getting hit in the head by the falling person. The receiving person on the end should reach for the falling person's shoulders, thus supporting his head and neck at the same time.

Rules: When the person is ready to fall back he says, "Falling," and the people behind him reply, "Fall on," and he begins to fall back. The team of three people stand still with their knees bent and their legs apart, with one foot slightly behind the other in a *bracing stance*. They begin catching the person when he reaches their chest area. (The participant should only fall back about two feet before being caught.) The team that is catching the participant does so with their arms outstretched and their palms extended out. As soon as they come in contact with him, they bend their knees in a downward motion, keeping their backs straight.

Preparation: This activity should be taken seriously by all participants or not done at all. The facilitator should be firm and direct when enforcing this rule. Once the *fall on* statement has been said by the receiving team, there is no joking around or all trust is gone.

Location: Outdoors on a level area. No chairs, tables, stools, or stumps should be used to elevate the falling participant off the ground—his feet should remain on the ground during the entire activity.

Number of Participants: A team of four participants

Age Range: 16 and older

Discussion Points: After the game, the facilitator should ask the following questions: What was fearful about this activity and how was that fear overcome? Was it scarier falling or catching someone? What type of team unity occurred during this activity?

Safety Precautions: All participants should take off any jewelry from their neck, wrists, ears, or fingers prior to this activity. The person falling should cross his arms over his chest to prevent him from hitting the people catching him as he falls. Once the team has caught the individual, they should raise him gently back up to a standing position. Teams should be selected with participants of approximately the same size and weight.

2

Innovation Games

Game #13: Water Balloons and Chopsticks

Objective: To teach personal accountability toward the team

Goals of Participants: To pick up a water balloon with chopsticks without breaking the water balloon

Overview: The team sits in a circle on the ground facing each other. In the middle of the circle is a plate with a water balloon on it. The first person in the group picks the water balloon up off the plate with his chopsticks, holds it for 15 seconds, and then sets it back down. The second person then picks up the balloon with his chopsticks, holds it for 15 seconds, and sets it back down. This pattern continues until the water balloon has been passed completely around the circle and placed back onto the plate in the center of the circle.

Rules: If the water balloon breaks during the game, the group is given another balloon and resumes play. After the first round of the game is played, two more rounds should be played so team members become more familiar with using the chopsticks and so they gain more confidence.

Preparation: The facilitator needs a water balloon (with enough spares to last for three rounds) and a pair of chopsticks for each member of the team.

Location: Indoors or outdoors

Number of Participants: A team of up to five players

Age Range: Six and older

Discussion Points: After the game, the facilitator should ask the following questions: Did you feel accountable to the team as you performed the assigned task without breaking the water balloon? What innovative methods were used as you tried to improve your skills with the chopsticks during the second and third rounds of the game?

Safety Precautions: Participants should be spread out far enough in the circle so no risk of poking anyone or coming in contact with other team members is involved as they attempt to pick up the water balloon with their chopsticks.

Game #14: Balancing Nails

Objective: To use innovation and creative thinking to solve a puzzle

Goals of Participants: To stack 10 nails on the head of a standing nail in five minutes or less

Overview: The team is given 10 duplex nails to attempt to stack on the head of a nail that has been hammered into a piece of wood. The group has five minutes to complete the task.

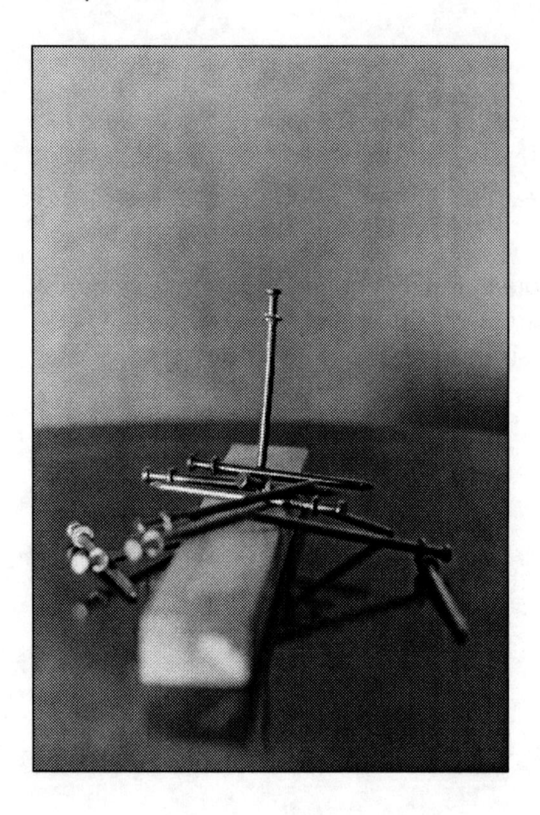

Rules: The facilitator should wait until the group has time to think of ways to solve this puzzle on their own before giving the following solution: The first nail is laid on the end of the standing nail horizontally, and then eight nails are placed diagonally on the horizontal nail, alternating right and left sides hanging down with the heads above the horizontal nail. The last nail is placed on top horizontally next to the heads of the eight diagonal nails to "lock in" these nails just under the heads.

Preparation: The facilitator needs one duplex nail driven with a hammer into one six-inch-long piece of wood that is two inches wide and 10 duplex nails for the puzzle.

Location: Indoors on a level table

Number of Participants: A team of five participants

Age Range: 10 and older

Discussion Points: After the game, the facilitator should ask the following question: How did you contribute innovative ideas to solve this puzzle?

Safety Precautions: The facilitator should keep track of the nails at all times to prevent personal injury or property damage.

Game #15: Balloon and Razor Game

Objective: To teach innovative leadership by having a team member lead someone in accomplishing a delicate task that will have immediate consequences if it is done too hastily

Goals of Participants: To carefully work together as quickly as possible to shave a balloon without popping it

Overview: The team is divided into pairs with one person blindfolded and the other person holding an air-filled balloon covered in shaving cream. The blindfolded partner attempts to shave the balloon with the directions of his partner who is holding the balloon.

Rules: This event is timed, and the pair with the best time removing all of the shaving cream off the balloon wins the event.

Preparation: Each pair receives an air-filled 12-inch balloon covered with shaving cream which the facilitator prepares prior to the game, a disposable razor, and a blindfold. Each pair needs a small bucket of water to clean the shaving cream off during the game.

Location: Indoors or outdoors

Number of Participants: A group of at least five pairs

Age Range: Eight and older

Discussion Points: After the game, the facilitator should ask the following questions: In what ways did you and your partner succeed in this event even if you did not win? What were some creative directions that your partner gave while you were shaving the balloon to ensure that all of the shaving cream was cleared off without popping the balloon?

Safety Precautions: The blindfolded person should use caution in holding a sharp razor during the entire activity.

Game #16: Marble Spin

Objective: To demonstrate how individual performance impacts the team's overall success

Goals of Participants: To spin a marble in a large, upside-down traffic cone for as long as possible

Overview: One at a time, team members are timed to see how long they can keep a marble spinning in an upside-down traffic cone without stopping or having the marble fall out of the small opening at the bottom of the cone. The accumulative individual times are added up for an overall team score. The team competes with itself in two additional rounds of the game to attempt to improve its accumulative time.

Rules: Each participant places a marble in the cone and starts spinning the cone as fast as he can. As soon as the marble stops, so does the time. That participant's name and time are written down on a pad of paper to be added up after everyone on the team takes a turn.

Preparation: The facilitator needs one traffic cone, one small marble, a stopwatch, a pencil, and a pad of paper.

Location: Indoors or outdoors

Number of Participants: A team of 5 to 10 participants

Age Range: Eight and older

Discussion Points: After the game, the facilitator should ask the following questions: Did you feel pressure in performing your task, knowing that the team was depending on you? Is this type of accountability good? What are some examples in life where this type of responsibility is placed on individuals?

Safety Precautions: Participants should be spread out far enough to not come in contact with each other during the game.

Game #17: Ladder Ball

Objective: To develop problem-solving skills as a team

Goals of Participants: To hold a wooden ladder off the ground in order to move two large exercise balls

Overview: The team holds a small, wooden ladder horizontally and three feet off the ground, with half of the group on one end and half on the other. Sitting on each end of the ladder is a large exercise ball. The team stands with their feet stationary and attempts to exchange the two balls to the opposite sides of the ladder without the balls touching any person or the ground.

Rules: If a ball falls off the ladder, the team starts over with both balls back at the starting point.

Preparation: The facilitator needs a small, wooden bunk-bed-type ladder and two exercise balls.

Location: Outdoors or indoors

Number of Participants: A team of two to four participants

Age Range: Eight and older

Discussion Points: After the game, the facilitator should ask the following questions: What inventive ways did the team use to solve this challenge? What would you do differently if you had another chance? The facilitator may want to give the team another chance to apply what they learned.

Safety Precautions: All members of the team and those watching should be alert during the game to avoid being hit with the ladder or the balls.

Game #18: Human Wheelbarrow Obstacle Course

Objective: To teach creative cooperation as each person relies on a partner to complete a task

Goals of Participants: To navigate through a ball obstacle course with the help of another team member

Overview: In teams consisting of two people, each team travels through an obstacle course where dozens of tennis and golf balls are laid on the ground. One person is held up by his legs in a wheelbarrow fashion by his partner and attempts to walk on his hands through the balls. Both the wheelbarrow participant and his partner walk through the course without touching any of the balls. After the team has crossed the course, they trade places and cross the course again.

Rules: If either person touches a ball with his hands or feet, the team has to start the game over. To add to the fun of this activity, several two-man teams should attempt this task at the same time going in opposite directions.

Preparation: The obstacle course should be made with 50 or more golf and tennis balls on the grass, with a long rope laid on the ground to determine the boundary of the course.

Location: Outdoors

Number of Participants: Five two-person teams

Age Range: Five and older

Discussion Points: After the game, the facilitator should ask the following questions: What did you learn about your partner after attempting this course? What was hard about this game and what was easy?

Safety Precautions: The person walking should be very observant to avoid stepping on the hands of a wheelbarrow participant on another team. This person should also steer his own wheelbarrow participant away from other teams to avoid colliding into them.

Game #19: Tennis Ball Canoe

Objective: To use innovative methods to "reinvent the wheel" in transporting team members

Goals of Participants: To work together to move two team members using resources the facilitator gives them

Overview: A team works together to transport a piece of plywood holding two people for a distance of 25 feet by rolling the plywood on tennis balls. The two people sitting on the plywood each have a canoe paddle and they paddle against the ground to propel themselves forward. The other team members are either pushing the plywood ahead or gathering the tennis balls that have traveled underneath the back end of the plywood and placing them underneath the front end of the plywood so the plywood is constantly moving forward.

Rules: If the plywood falls off the tennis balls or a rider falls off the plywood, the team has to go back to the starting area and begin the journey again.

Preparation: The facilitator needs 100 tennis balls, a piece of thick plywood large enough for two participants to ride on, two canoe paddles, and cones for the starting and finish lines.

Location: Outdoors on a grassy field

Number of Participants: A team of five participants

Age Range: Eight and older

Discussion Points: After the game, the facilitator should ask the following questions: What strategies were used to accomplish this task? How did team members strengthen their relationship with each other as a result of this game?

Safety Precautions: The team members pushing the plywood should be cautioned not to go too fast and risk injuring the riders or the person gathering the tennis balls. The two people riding the plywood should be careful when paddling to avoid coming in contact with team members pushing the plywood.

Game #20: Pass the Potato

Objective: To demonstrate the concept of "strength in numbers"

Goals of Participants: To move a potato 10 feet using only plastic cocktail swords

Overview: The facilitator places a potato on a table and gives each team member a plastic cocktail sword. He then asks one team member to pick up and carry the potato 10 feet, using only his cocktail sword. The participant pokes his sword into the potato (usually only going a third of the length of the blade) and tries to lift it off the table at least 12 inches. Typically, the weight of the potato will break the sword. The facilitator then asks two people to work together to attempt to pick up the potato using their cocktail swords. If they are unsuccessful, the facilitator continues to add more people and resources (i.e., swords) until the task is complete. In most cases, it takes the entire team to transport the potato.

Rules: The potato must be lifted at least 12 inches. Only the sword is to be used to lift and transport the potato. If a participant tries to lift the potato with his hands or cradle it against his fingers or arms, he is asked to try again using only the plastic sword to touch the potato.

Preparation: The facilitator needs one large potato and a package of plastic cocktail swords.

Location: Indoors or outdoors

Number of Participants: A team of five people

Age Range: Eight and older

Discussion Points: After the game, the facilitator should ask the following questions: Why was accomplishing this task easier when more people helped? What are examples of tasks in life that become easier when more people contribute?

Safety Precautions: Participants should use caution when handling the plastic swords to avoid injuring themselves or others.

Game #21: Crepe Paper Grid

Objective: To develop listening skills among team members

Goals of Participants: To walk blindfolded while being verbally guided by a partner through a grid of crepe paper toward a finish line

Overview: The team is divided into pairs where one person coaches his blindfolded partner though a grid of crepe paper that is taped to the walls and is two feet off the ground. The grid should be an eight-by-eight foot square with at least four lines crisscrossing each other. (This requirement can be modified to fit the dimensions of the room.) The person traveling through the grid should do so without breaking the crepe paper. The blindfolded person can touch the paper grid, just not break it.

Rules: The person coaching the blindfolded participant should stand at the edge of the grid to give instructions. If the person breaks the paper grid then he has to return to the starting area and begin again after the grid is repaired. Depending on the room size, multiple teams can play simultaneously.

Preparation: The facilitator needs crepe paper and masking tape. The crepe paper lines should be strung tightly from the walls.

Location: Indoors

Number of Participants: Up to four two-man teams

Age Range: Eight and older

Discussion Points: After the game, the facilitator should ask the following questions: What listening techniques were used by the blindfolded person? What creative ways were used by both the coach and the blindfolded player to avoid breaking the crepe paper? If multiple teams played, what methods were used by the blindfolded participant to block out distractions made by other coaches to only listen to his coach?

Safety Precautions: Chairs, tables, and other tripping hazards should be removed from the room prior to this activity.

Game #22: Blindfolded Leaky Backpack

Objective: To teach the importance of following directions given by team members

Goals of Participants: To find the spilled contents of a backpack while blindfolded

Overview: One blindfolded team member attempts to gather 12 items to fill a backpack while following the prompts of team members who can see the items. The blindfolded participant holds a small backpack and walks slowly along a 15-foot-long narrow pathway gathering up all the items on both sides of the path and placing them in his backpack.

Rules: The assisting team members can only give the following verbal cues: "Hot" (if the participant is in very close proximity to an item), "Warm" (if he gets near an item), and "Cold" (if he is far away from one of the items). If the blindfolded participant receives the verbal cue that he is warm but he distances himself from the item in an attempt to find it, the team can yell, "Cold," to indicate that he has gone the wrong way and then affirm by saying, "Warm" or even "Hot," if he corrects his direction and advances toward the item.

Preparation: The facilitator needs a backpack, a blindfold, and 12 small camping items (e.g., a flashlight, compass, water bottle, first aid kit, sunscreen, poncho, bandanna, whistle, bottle of hand sanitizer, mess kit, bag of trail mix, and a deck of playing cards).

Location: Outdoors on a trail

Number of Participants: A team of at least five participants

Age Range: Six and older

Discussion Points: After the game, the facilitator should ask the following questions: While blindfolded, how clear were the directions that were being given to you? What was the hardest item to find and why?

Safety Precautions: The facilitator is responsible for finding a section of the trail that is free from tripping hazards or any poisonous or thorny plants to avoid injuring the blindfolded participant.

Game #23: Sticky Delivery

Objective: To collectively strategize and implement a plan in order to solve a task that impacts the entire team

Goals of Participants: To move as a team from one location to another while being physically connected to each other

Overview: Before starting the game, the facilitator should set up the following scenario: "About 10 minutes ago, the entire team was in a delivery truck that was traveling down the street to deliver glue to an elementary school when the driver of the truck had to slam on the breaks to avoid an accident. The truck did successfully avoid the accident; however, as a result of the sudden stop, all of the glue came out of the bottles and covered all of the team members. The team was quick to leave the vehicle safely, but in doing so they all became glued to each other. A member of the team notices a water hose 25 feet away that each person can use to wash off the glue and separate himself from the rest of the team." So, as a team, they must walk (while being tied together) 25 feet until they reach the imaginary water hose.

Rules: After the scenario is read, the facilitator ties all of the team members' hands and legs together with bandannas to form the group into a circle before the team sets out on their journey toward the finish line. The team must move slowly so that no one trips or too much pressure is put on an individual's hands or legs. The team can stop at any time during the game to make adjustments to the bandannas.

Preparation: The facilitator needs four bandannas per person and two cones for the finish line.

Location: Outdoors on a grassy field

Number of Participants: A team of five participants

Age Range: Eight and older

Discussion Points: After the game, the facilitator should ask the following questions: Who was the leader and why did that person become the leader? What elements of innovation were used to accomplish this task (e.g., creativity, inspiration, strategic planning, problem solving)?

Safety Precautions: The bandannas should not be tied too tightly—the participant should be able to move without discomfort. The team should walk or crawl at the same time to ensure that no one is being dragged along. The facilitator and other leaders should serve as spotters to assist each participant in keeping his balance.

3

Cooperation Games

Game #24: Salt Shaker Relay

Objective: To build team spirit and good sportsmanship while competing against another team

Goals of Participants: To communicate to fellow team members faster than the opposing team

Overview: Two teams of 10 people per team sit on opposite sides of a long picnic table. At one end of the table, one person from each team focuses on the facilitator as he flips a coin. Everyone else focuses on a salt shaker that is sitting on the opposite end of the table. Participants on each team hold hands with fellow teammates during the game. The two opposing teammates that are watching the facilitator have the responsibility of squeezing the person's hand next to them when they see the coin land on *heads*. If the leader flips the coin and it lands on *tails*, nothing happens. When the coin lands on heads, the hand squeezes continue from one person to the next until the last person in the line attempts to grab the salt shaker before his opponent does.

Rules: The person that grabs the salt shaker first now rotates to the front of his line where the facilitator is and everyone else slides down one position. The team to be first in rotating all of their members to the front of the line wins the game.

Preparation: The facilitator needs a plastic salt shaker and a coin. A large indoor table or a large outdoor picnic table is also needed.

Location: Indoors or outdoors

Number of Participants: Two teams of 10 people

Age Range: Six and older

Discussion Points: After the game, the facilitator should ask the following questions: How did your team unite in competing against the other team? What methods were used to show respect for the other team in either winning or losing the game?

Safety Precautions: To prevent hand injuries, the participant that is reaching for the salt shaker should be warned to use caution when reacting quickly, thus avoiding jamming his hand into the side of the table while attempting to grab the salt shaker. Participants should also be cautioned not to squeeze each other's hands too hard.

Game #25: Five

Objective: To develop competition and cooperation at the same time with other players who are seeking to accomplish the same objective

Goals of Participants: To advance to each of the five levels to become one of the five winners

Overview: A group of 20 people compete to be the first five people to get to level five by beating five different opponents at the game Rock Paper Scissors. Each time a participant wins a game, he advances to another level by seeking out another player who won his round. When a participant reaches level five, he shouts out the word *five* five times. The game is over when five people shout out.

Rules: When someone loses a round of Rock Paper Scissors, he should immediately stand at the edge of the playing area so the focus remains on the participants that are still competing. Those players that are still competing should move in closer to the center of the playing area each time they advance in the game.

Preparation: The facilitator may need to remind the participants on the following rules of Rock Paper Scissors: Each participant finds another player and both people face each other and stamp their right fist three times into their left hand which is upturned with the fingers extended. On the third stamp of the fist, each person makes a hand gesture of rock (closed fist), paper (hand face down with the fingers extended), or scissors (index and middle fingers shaped like scissors). The person wins if he has rock over scissors, paper over rock, or scissors over paper.

Location: Indoors or outdoors

Number of Participants: A group of 20 people

Age Range: Eight and older

Discussion Points: After the game, the facilitator should ask the following questions: What did cooperation mean in this game? How was cooperation used and how was competition used to determine the winning team of five players?

Safety Precautions: A large playing area is needed so as people are quickly moving around, they do not collide into each other.

Game #26: Broom Hockey

Objective: To build esprit de corps among teammates and respect for their competitors

Goals of Participants: To win the game of hockey as a team

Overview: Two teams of six players play a game of hockey in an outdoor paved area using brooms for hockey sticks and a tennis ball for a puck. One of the players on each team serves as a goalie and guards the goal, which is set off by traffic cones on both sides of the playing area. Three other players serve as forwards and two others as defensemen. The game is timed with three periods of 15 minutes, and the team with the highest score at the end of the third period is the winner.

Rules: The facilitator serves as the referee and blows the whistle to stop play when the ball goes out-of-bounds, when someone kicks or body-blocks the ball, or when a goal is scored. The game stops until the referee blows the whistle to resume the game. At the beginning of each period a face-off is conducted, where the referee stands between two players facing each other and drops the ball at their feet. Both players attempt to gain possession of the ball or pass it to a teammate.

Preparation: The facilitator needs four cones for the two goals, a tennis ball (with spares), a whistle, a stopwatch, and one broom for each player.

Location: A large outdoor playing area enclosed by a fence

Number of Participants: Two teams of six players

Age Range: 12 and older

Discussion Points: After the game, the facilitator should ask the following questions: What position did you play? What influence did you have to help your team try to win the game? Then the facilitator can discuss the importance of responsibility and accountability that each player has in helping the team succeed.

Safety Precautions: Penalties should not be tolerated at all by the referee—any player that is caught exerting too much physical contact such as body checking, elbowing, high-sticking (i.e., holding the stick waist-high), or striking an opponent with a stick is out of the game or the entire game stops.

Game #27: Name That Answer

Objective: To promote unity as a team while benefiting from the experiences of team members and competitors

Goals of Participants: To display more creativity than another team in answering questions that will be judged

Overview: The facilitator gives both teams an identical list of partial questions that each team has to collectively choose the most clever answers for. Each answer has to be a true experience from at least one person on the team. The team brainstorms what the second part of the question might be and comes up with possible answers. This process takes about 30 minutes to go through the entire list. Then, one question at a time, the facilitator holds up a poster of what the second half of the question is. One person from the team has 25 seconds to choose one of the team's answers. For each question, another person from the team chooses an answer from the list of team members' experiences.

First Part of the Question	*Second Part of the Question*
Name the juiciest	dessert you ever had
Name the hairiest	pet you ever owned
Name the scariest	birthday present you ever received
Name the tallest	glass of soda you ever drank
Name the biggest	cookie you ever ate
Name the longest	distance you ever ran
Name the meanest	animal you saw at the zoo
Name the goofiest	T-shirt you ever saw
Name the kindest	act of service you ever performed
Name the coldest	place you went on a vacation to
Name the hardest	hike you ever took
Name the happiest	place on earth
Name the cleanest	place in your bedroom
Name the messiest	meal you ever ate
Name the shortest	test you ever took
Name the fastest	restaurant to get a hamburger
Name the noisiest	appliance in your kitchen
Name the saddest	day of your last summer vacation
Name the hottest	snack food you ever tasted
Name the smallest	car you ever saw

Rules: A panel of three judges will listen to the answers from both teams and choose which one they like better (based on creativity and truthfulness). Each answer the judges choose is worth one point for that team. At the end of the 20 questions, the team with the most points wins the game.

Preparation: The facilitator prepares the first half of the questions and gives each team a copy of the list. Then, the second half of each question is written on a separate poster board. The facilitator also needs the help of three people to serve as judges.

Location: Indoors or outdoors

Number of Participants: Two teams of 10 people per team

Age Range: 12 and older

Discussion Points: After the game, the facilitator can discuss the answers given by team members as a way to illustrate how a varied background of experiences can strengthen a team and help it succeed.

Safety Precautions: Answers should be appropriate, respectful, and unoffensive—judges should penalize teams with such answers with a loss of points.

Game #28: Broomstick and Bucket Game

Objective: To teach resourcefulness and instill team spirit as each person competes against an opponent on behalf of his team

Goals of Participants: To be the first person to retrieve a bucket using a broomstick

Overview: Two teams are organized to compete against each other. Each person on the team is paired up with a competitor from the other team to be the first person to pick up a wooden bucket with a broomstick. These two participants stand facing each other, each holding a broomstick, with a wooden bucket between them on the ground. The first one to successfully pick up the bucket by its handle receives one point for his team. When everyone on the team has participated, the team with the highest score wins the game.

Rules: The broomstick can be used for retrieving the bucket or blocking the opponent's stick as he attempts to retrieve the bucket.

Preparation: The facilitator needs two wooden broomsticks and a wooden bucket with a rope handle for each pair of participants.

Location: Outdoors

Number of Participants: Two five-person teams

Age Range: Eight and older

Discussion Points: After the game, the facilitator should ask the following question: What types of feelings did you have during this activity in bearing the responsibility of earning points for your team?

Safety Precautions: The facilitator should monitor this game closely to ensure that the broomsticks are used properly to avoid any injuries.

Game #29: Milk Can and Softball Toss

Objective: To promote positive team communication that will increase individual performance and concentration

Goals of Participants: To toss a softball into an old-fashioned milk can

Overview: Three teams of five people per team compete against each other to maintain the highest score. Each person starts out with 100 points. Each player gets 10 attempts to toss a softball into a milk can. Each time he misses the can, 10 points are subtracted from his score. The team with the highest number of points wins the game.

Rules: One at a time, each participant takes his turn from the same starting point, which is six feet away from the milk can. A scorekeeper is needed to keep track of the points for the three teams.

Preparation: The facilitator needs at least three softballs and an old-fashioned milk can. One player from each team should also be asked to gather up the balls that missed the can.

Location: Outdoors

Number of Participants: Three teams of five players each

Age Range: Eight and older

Discussion Points: Prior to this game, the facilitator should point out the special feature of the scoring on this game, which is to start with a high score and decrease it when individuals miss the goal. After the game, the facilitator should ask the following questions: Did the scoring system promote better performance and accountability or did it cause tension in the team and too much pressure for the players? If tension was felt among the team, what efforts, if any, did team members make to encourage positive communication and support despite lower scores? What would the team have done differently if given the chance to play the game over?

Safety Precautions: If the milk can is old or weathered, it may be rusty. Caution should be used in handling it to prevent individuals from being cut on its sharp edges.

Game #30: Midnight Football

Objective: To create unity as a team as individual performances determine whether the team succeeds during a series of uncommon tests

Goals of Participants: To advance a football toward the end zone to score

Overview: Two teams compete in an adapted game of football in an indoor setting. Both teams crawl on the floor for the entire time trying to advance a foam football toward their end zone. This game is offensive play only—no physical contact between teams is allowed. The defensive team only tries to obtain the ball when it is passed or fumbled. The game is played in the dark. The facilitator stands next to the light switch and turns the lights off and on randomly. When the lights are off, the play begins with the team in possession of the ball advancing toward their end zone. As soon as the lights go back on, the play immediately stops.

Rules: When the lights go on, everyone has to freeze in place and stay completely still. For the offensive team, if someone is still moving, the penalty is that the ball changes possession to the other team. If a member of the defensive team is moving, the penalty is that the entire defensive team goes back to the other team's end zone. If players from both teams are caught moving, then the ball is taken back 10 feet and the offensive team maintains possession of the ball. Once the lights go out and it is dark, the game resumes until the lights are turned on again. The first team with the highest score after 20 minutes of play wins the game.

Preparation: The facilitator needs a foam football. The facilitator also serves as the referee to determine if any players move while the lights are on.

Location: Indoors in a gym

Number of Participants: Two teams of five players

Age Range: 12 and older

Discussion Points: After the game, the facilitator should ask the following questions: How would you evaluate your team's ability to stop play and freeze when the lights came on? Were team players unified in this rule or did it cause frustration when the team was penalized because of the actions of certain players? How can this frustration dissolve and unity fill its place? What can the team do to help teammates improve their performance?

Safety Precautions: The room should provide a large, open area that is free of chairs and tables in order to prevent injuries. With the lights out, players should use caution and crawl slowly to avoid colliding into each other.

Game #31: Stick Pull

Objective: To build friendships and promote sportsmanship through competition

Goals of Participants: To pull a stick harder than an opponent

Overview: Two participants sit down on the grass facing each other, with a heavy-duty wooden handle between them. Both players line up their legs directly across from each other to provide leverage as each participant attempts to pull the wooden handle toward himself. As the players begin, both participants grip the handle with their palms down and their fingers wrapped around the handle. One participant places his hands close together in the middle of the handle and the other person places his hands on both sides of his opponent's hands.

Rules: The winner of the game is the one who pulls his opponent over toward him, lifting him off the ground.

Preparation: The facilitator needs a heavy-duty wooden handle (e.g., from a broom, rake, or shovel).

Location: Outdoors on a grassy field

Number of Participants: Two players

Age Range: 12 and older

Discussion Points: After the game, the facilitator should ask the following questions: Was good sportsmanship used during this activity? What character strengths and attributes of the other person did each player learn as a result of this game? What elements of respect were displayed during this game?

Safety Precautions: To avoid injuries, participants should be cautioned prior to the game that once the winner has pulled his opponent off the ground, he is to gently lower him down to the ground and not attempt to pull him completely over.

Game #32: Grass Stain Tag

Objective: To get to know different team members as much as possible in a quickly changing environment

Goals of Participants: To avoid being tagged while getting to know other team members

Overview: A large group of people lie on their stomachs in a circle with their heads pointing toward the center of the circle. From this position, each person is paired off in a smaller team of two people that hold hands. A large gap should be left between each pair. Two people in the group do not lie down, but they start a game of tag. One of these participants is "it," and he chases the other person, trying to tag him before he joins another team that is lying on the ground. As soon as this person joins a team, the team member on the opposite edge has to leave by standing up and running to another team without getting caught by the person that is "it." Throughout the game, the paired players lying on the ground should ask each other discovery-type questions such as: What is your name? Where are you from? How many times have you been to camp? What have you done recently that is really cool?

Rules: When a person is tagged by the person that is "it," that participant is now "it" and does the chasing after he counts to 10 to avoid retagging the other person too quickly.

Preparation: The facilitator needs a large grassy playing area for this game.

Location: Outdoors

Number of Participants: A team of 20 players

Age Range: Eight and older

Discussion Points: After the game, the facilitator should ask the following questions: How many different teams were you on? What interesting facts did you learn about team members as you got to know new people during the game?

Safety Precautions: The person that is "it" does the chasing at the feet, not the heads, of the group that is lying on their stomachs. The circle that the group forms should be large enough with plenty of gaps between each team so that no participant gets stepped on by the person that is "it" or the person he is chasing.

Game #33: Backward Crab Relay

Objective: To demonstrate how individual performance affects the entire team

Goals of Participants: To race in relay fashion, going backward in a crab-like position

Overview: Five-person teams run individual races against the participants from other teams from the starting line back to the finish line, racing backward in a crab-like position. (Each racer lies with his back off the ground, being supported by his arms and legs as he attempts to crawl backward toward the finish line and back to the starting area, which is 16 feet in total distance.)

Rules: If a team member falls down as he crawls backward, he can resume his position and continue the race. Once a participant arrives back at the finish line, he tags the next player to continue the next leg of the race. This pattern continues until the fifth participant completes the race. The first team to have all five participants complete the course is the winner.

Preparation: The facilitator needs cones to designate a starting line and a finish line.

Location: Outdoors on a grassy field

Number of Participants: At least four five-person teams

Age Range: Eight and older

Discussion Points: After the game, the facilitator should ask the following questions: How did cooperation and competition help unify the team as each person performed this difficult task?

Safety Precautions: Players should stretch prior to the race and should use caution not to hyperextend their arms or legs.

Game #34: Fishbowl Challenge

Objective: To promote a sense of camaraderie as teams compete in a race to win the event

Goals of Participants: To work together to be the first team to score 50 points

Overview: Each three-person team drops a pair of dice into a fishbowl full of water and records the numbers, attempting to be the first team to reach 50 points. One person on each team drops the dice into the water, one person grabs the dice out of the water, and one person writes down the points on a notepad.

Rules: The dice have to land on the bottom of the bowl before the dice can be read. If two (or more) teams reach 50 points at the same time, the water level is the tiebreaker. The team that has lost the least amount of water at the end of the activity wins the game.

Preparation: The facilitator needs a pair of dice, a notepad, a pencil, and a glass fishbowl (uniform in size) for each team. Each fishbowl should be filled with the same amount of water. A ruler is needed to measure the water level before and after the game.

Location: Indoors or outdoors

Number of Participants: Four teams of three people per team

Age Range: Six and older

Discussion Points: After the game, the facilitator should ask the following questions: How did your team keep a balance of speed in grabbing the dice out of the bowl to try again while maintaining the high water level in order to succeed in this game? What, if anything, did your team learn from the competition that you would apply if you had to perform this task again?

Safety Precautions: Caution should be used in handling the glass fishbowls.

Game #35: Wallyball

Objective: To increase team unity and communication by using additional resources in playing a combination game of volleyball and racquetball

Goals of Participants: To win a game of volleyball by using the walls and the ceiling

Overview: In a racquetball court, two teams of six participants play a modified form of volleyball. When the serving team serves the ball, the ball cannot hit the back wall or the ceiling. However, the receiving team can use their back wall and ceiling in returning the ball. The side walls on both sides of the net can be played by both teams as long as the ball is hit by different players only three times on their side of the court.

Rules: Scoring only occurs when the serving team serves the ball clearly over the net and the receiving team fails to return the ball back over. The first team to reach 25 points with a two-point lead wins the game. No participant can touch the net as he attempts to either advance the ball over the net or block his opponent's ball. The ball can be recovered from the net during play and counts as one of the team's hits. The ball is out-of-bounds when it hits the ceiling or back wall of the opponent's court or when it hits two or more walls consecutively during play.

Preparation: The facilitator needs a wallyball net and a wallyball. (A volleyball can be used.)

Location: A special adapted racquetball court with ringlets to hang the wallyball net

Number of Participants: Two teams of six players

Age Range: 12 and older

Discussion Points: After the game, the facilitator should ask the following questions: How did using additional resources such as the walls and ceiling help your team in competing? What additional communication was required with the game of wallyball in order to take full advantage of the extra resources?

Safety Precautions: Players should not spike the ball into their opponent's court. Participants should be alert and aware of where the ball is at all times to avoid being accidently hit during the game.

Game #36: Tin Can Tower

Objective: To teach that overcoming obstacles is a part of completing important tasks

Goals of Participants: To work as a team to stack a tower of tin cans in the middle of the playing area while simultaneously using playground balls to attempt to knock down the other team's tower

Overview: Each team is given eight empty tin cans to try to stack in two tiers while playing a game of dodgeball with an opposing team that is positioned 15 feet away. In addition to trying to hit opposing players with the balls, participants attempt to knock down the opposing team's tower. If a participant is hit or if his throw is caught by an opponent, he sits out of the game in an imaginary jail that is set up alongside the playing area.

Rules: The way that a participant can reenter the game from the jail area is if all eight cans from his team's tower are formed for five seconds before being knocked down or if a fellow team player catches an opponent's ball. One point is awarded to each team any time the tin-can tower is formed and no team members are in jail. The first team to reach 10 points wins the game.

Preparation: The facilitator needs 16 tin cans (#10 size) and 10 playground balls.

Location: Outdoors on a basketball court with each team sectioned off on opposite sides of the court

Number of Participants: Two teams of 12 players

Age Range: 12 and older

Discussion Points: After the game, the facilitator should ask both teams: What strategies did your team use to overcome the obstacles provided by the opposing team? He should ask the winning team: What methods did you use to accomplish the two tasks of building the tower and keeping team members in the game?

Safety Precautions: Participants should be cautioned prior to the game not to aim for an opponent's head and neck area when throwing the ball.

4

Communication Games

Game #37: Mousetrap

Objective: To develop communication skills and deductive reasoning

Goals of Participants: To make decisions based on the interactions of each character in a hypothetical story as played out in each round of the game

Overview: Before starting the game, the facilitator should set up the following scenario: A group of mice live in the country where they eat the grain of several farmers. The farmers have banded together to attempt to solve this problem, and each night they place mousetraps out to catch the mice. Every night, a different mouse is trapped in a mousetrap. The mice are concerned about the traps and have enlisted the help of the mice police and a mouse doctor. The mice police try to identify which farmer is involved in the trapping of mice, and the mouse doctor tries to help the mice that have been harmed in a trap.

A group of 20 people sit in a circle, and each person is given a different colored playing card that only he is able to look at. The color of the card will determine the type of role each person plays in the game. If the card is green, that player is a mouse; if the card is red, that player is a farmer; if the card is black, that player is one of the mice police; and if the card is yellow, that player is the mouse doctor. Fourteen green cards, three red cards, two black cards, and one yellow card are given out by the facilitator of the game.

Rules: The facilitator stands at the front of the circle and has everyone place their heads down with their eyes closed. Then, the facilitator asks the participants that have red cards (the farmers) to lift their heads up and choose one of the participants who still have their heads down to be the mouse they remove from the game. (When a player is removed from the game, he still sits in the circle, but he cannot talk or participate for the rest of the activity.)

Then, the farmers put their heads down with their eyes closed and the facilitator asks the participants that have black cards (the mice police) to lift their heads up and point to one person in the group that they suspect is a farmer. The facilitator responds by nodding his head either *yes* or *no*. The mice police are asked to put their heads down with their eyes closed and the facilitator asks the one participant that has a yellow card (the mouse doctor) to lift his head up and pick one person to rescue (without knowing if the person is a mouse or a farmer).

Next, the facilitator asks everyone to lift their heads up, and he tells the group the story of how one of the mice got stuck in a mousetrap during the night and was removed from the game. (Unless the mouse doctor randomly picked that person and saved him.) Then, the entire group votes on one other person who they collectively assume is a farmer from the group that should also be removed from the game for his use of mousetraps. This stage is where the mice police try to persuade others to vote if they know who the farmer is from the silent conversation they had with the facilitator. The mice police should be careful not to let on that they know too much because their identities are secret and if the real farmers suspect one of the participants is one of the police, they may persuade others to vote him out from this round by accusing him of being a farmer. After this round, the same process happens again where the facilitator has everyone place their heads down with their eyes closed and he calls on each group to lift their heads at the appropriate time. The farmers choose another mouse, then the mice police choose another suspect, and the mouse doctor chooses someone that may be saved if he picks the person that the farmers had chosen to be in the mousetrap. The game continues until either all of the farmers are voted out of the game or the farmers remove all of the other participants.

Participants must listen carefully for clues and watch the body language of all players to come to the correct conclusion. The team dynamics may change during this game and loyalties and alliances may form that either help a participant succeed or cause him to be eliminated from the game. Thus, it is important that each participant watches the verbal and nonverbal expressions of each player.

Preparation: The facilitator needs a couple of decks of playing cards with red, black, green, and yellow colors in the deck such as Rook® cards.

Location: Indoors or outdoors

Number of Participants: A group of 20 people

Age Range: 12 and older

Discussion Points: After the game, the facilitator should discuss what transpired during the game and then ask the following questions: How were teams formed and alliances made? What was your role in the game and what different types of communication were you sending to other team members? Who was loyal to whom and why?

Safety Precautions: This game should be played in a fun and respectful environment. If the atmosphere becomes too dark or cynical where players feel uncomfortable or pressured, the facilitator should step in to make corrections.

Game #38: Pick-Up Sticks

Objective: To communicate effectively while working with another person

Goals of Participants: To win a game of pick-up sticks with a partner

Overview: The facilitator dumps five 12-count packages of colored pencils on the floor and jumbles up the pencils to form a heap. Then, he divides the group into teams of two people per team. Each pair is assigned one of the 12 pencil colors and is responsible for picking up all five pencils of that color from the pile without moving any of the other pencils. Both players need to be touching the same pencil the entire time as they attempt to withdraw it from the pile. Team members need to slowly work together and communicate constantly as they undertake this task.

Rules: The teams take turns, with each team removing one pencil per turn. If a team moves any pencil other than the one they are picking up, their turn is over and the next team attempts to remove one of their colored pencils. The first team to successfully remove all five pencils of their assigned color wins the game.

Preparation: The facilitator needs five 12-count packages of colored pencils.

Location: Indoors or outdoors

Number of Participants: Up to 12 teams (one for each pencil color in a 12-count package) of two people per team

Age Range: Eight and older

Discussion Points: After the game, the facilitator should ask the following questions: What was the hardest aspect of this game? Was there continuous communication between both team members? Did the communication help or not? Why?

Safety Precautions: Participants should use caution in playing with sharpened pencils.

Game #39: Soup Can Phones

Objective: To stress the importance of communicating in close proximity and having good listening skills. This activity is ideal at the beginning of an event where participants are still getting to know each other.

Goals of Participants: To make soup can phones and use them in teams of two

Overview: Each team makes a homemade phone by attaching the two ends of a piece of string to two soup cans. Then each team has a conversation using the phone while standing 10 feet away from each other.

Rules: The facilitator asks each person to discover five common experiences that he and his new friend share while talking on their homemade phones.

Preparation: The facilitator needs two clean, empty soup cans, 10 feet of balloon string, and a small cube of paraffin wax for each team. Before the activity, the facilitator should use a hammer and nail to punch a small hole in the top of each soup can. The balloon string also needs to be coated with wax.

Location: Indoors or outdoors

Number of Participants: Four teams of two people per team

Age Range: Six and older

Discussion Points: The facilitator can point out that this activity was an object lesson to illustrate four aspects that are important in the development of one-on-one friendships:

- Personal connection. Unplugged activities are needed every once in a while to build meaningful friendships, especially in a world of high-tech, impersonal connection.
- Close proximity. Nothing beats talking to someone in the same room, even if it is 10 feet away.
- Listening skills. These homemade phones really do allow sound waves to travel along the string, but it takes extra effort to listen in order to understand. The true lesson in listening is to *listen with the intent to understand*.
- Time. It only took a few minutes to make the phones and use them, but it was time well spent in accomplishing a task as a team.

Safety Precautions: The facilitator should make sure that each can has smooth edges.

Game #40: Name Associations, Animal Signs, and Team Cheers

Objective: To teach quick methods of name identification so a new team can become unified

Goals of Participants: To learn the names of team members and connect with each other by creating a team name and cheer

Overview: Each person on the team introduces himself and then associates one of his hobbies with his name so team members can remember his name. For example, if Jared likes to collect rocks, his name association could be "Rock'n Jared," or if Patricia likes to collect cow memorabilia and collectables, her name association could be "Cow Patty." Another way to remember names is to associate an animal sign with each name. Each person identifies himself with an animal that starts with the same letter of his first name and creates an animal sign, so throughout the event people remember his name and his animal sign. For example, Susan could be *Susan Snake* with the sign of her forearm moving back and forth like a snake; Mike could be *Mike Monkey* with the sign of him jumping up and down like a monkey; Alex could be *Alex Alligator* with the sign of him clapping both arms up and down for an alligator's mouth; or Rachel could be *Rachel Raccoon* with the sign of her making finger circles around both eyes.

Rules: Once the individuals on the team have learned each other's names, then the group can create a team name and cheer. For example, a team could be the "Cupcakes" with the following cheer: "Apple pie, apple pie, we think you are great, but we are the Cupcakes, and we take the cake!"

Preparation: The facilitator should be prepared to help team members with ideas for their names associations or animal signs.

Location: Indoors or outdoors

Number of Participants: At least one team of 15 people

Age Range: Six and older

Discussion Points: Much later after the game has concluded, the facilitator should ask for volunteers to attempt to recall team members' name associations and animal signs as a kind of test to see if these memory methods really worked.

Safety Precautions: Each person should come up with his own name association and animal sign or seek help from the facilitator to avoid being offended by team members' well-meaning suggestions such as *William Whale* or *Emerson Elephant*.

Game #41: Know the Pinecone

Objective: To focus on specific individual character qualities in order to recognize those qualities in a group setting

Goals of Participants: To remember as many features of a pinecone as possible

Overview: Each team member is given a pinecone to look at and study for five minutes so that when it is taken away and placed in a basket with other pinecones, he will be able to identify his own pinecone.

Rules: Once the basket has been filled with pinecones from all of the team members, the facilitator goes to another room and shuffles the pinecones around. This step makes it difficult for each player to sort through and find his pinecone.

Preparation: The facilitator needs a pinecone for each person and one basket for the team.

Location: Indoors or outdoors

Number of Participants: A group of up to 25 participants

Age Range: Six and older

Discussion Points: After the game, the facilitator should ask the following questions: What methods did each participant try to use to remember elements of his pinecone? How does this game relate to being a part of a team? What specific qualities should each person observe in other team members on the team that will help unite the group?

Safety Precautions: To avoid injuries, participants should be warned that the pinecones may be prickly on the edges or may cause slivers.

Game #42: Maypole

Objective: To increase the communication pattern among team members in creating a physical pattern as a result of working together

Goals of Participants: To weave ribbons on a maypole using the members of both teams

Overview: Using a commercial maypole, the group divides into two smaller teams. The two teams form a circle around the pole with a member of each team alternating every other position with that of the other team. One team faces one direction in the circle and the other team faces the opposite direction. Each person grabs a different color of ribbon.

Rules: Half of the team rotates clockwise, alternating either raising each of their ribbons for another person to go under or lowering their ribbons to go under a member of the other team's ribbon. At the same time, the other team is walking counterclockwise, alternating the same pattern. In order to weave the pole successfully, both teams need to communicate and work together with each other by exercising give-and-take.

Preparation: The facilitator will need a commercial maypole with 12 ribbons that are each 14 feet in length and an assortment of colors.

Location: Outdoors

Number of Participants: Two smaller teams of six people each

Age Range: Six and older

Discussion Points: After the game, the facilitator should ask the following questions: Do you feel that both teams successfully completed the task? What did you learn in the process of weaving the ribbons? What types of communication methods where used during this activity?

Safety Precautions: The facilitator needs to ensure that the maypole is secure and will not tip over during the game.

Game #43: Backward Team Walk

Objective: To increase listening skills in order to overcome a challenge

Goals of Participants: To work in pairs to accomplish a task while walking backward

Overview: In teams of two, participants line up with their backs against each other, interlocking their elbows and bending their knees slightly. While in this stance, the team walks 25 feet to a cone with one person walking forward and the other person walking backward. When the team reaches the cone, they reverse roles and head back to the starting area.

Rules: During this game, each team member needs to constantly communicate his direction and speed of travel to his partner to avoid being disconnected. If the team does become disconnected, they need to return back to the starting area and start the course over again.

Preparation: The facilitator needs two cones—a starting cone and one that is placed 25 feet away.

Location: Outdoors

Number of Participants: Four small teams of two people each

Age Range: Eight and older

Discussion Points: After the game, the facilitator should ask the following questions: Did your team talk to one another during the entire course? If the answer is yes, how did that help you to stay unified and connected? If the answer is no, what could have happened to ensure better success? What situations in life are similar to participating in this game and how does constant communication help in those situations?

Safety Precautions: Participants should use caution and move slowly when walking backward to avoid tripping.

Game #44: Gold Mine

Objective: To teach listening skills and concise instruction delivery skills

Goals of Participants: To successfully complete a blindfolded walk with the help of a team member, while avoiding special pitfalls but also stepping on several plastic numbered spots in numeric order to accumulate points

Overview: The team divides into smaller teams of two people and approaches an imaginary gold mine tunnel, which is so dark that one member of the team is blindfolded so he cannot see. His partner becomes an imaginary flashlight and stands by the blindfolded player. The "flashlight" can see but has to communicate with walking instructions for his blindfolded partner to navigate through the tunnel, avoiding "pitfalls," which are tennis balls, while purposely stepping on numbered spots, which represent "gold deposits."

Rules: The number on the spots range from 1 to 10 with the number representing its dollar worth in millions (e.g., the number one spot represents one million dollars). The numbered spots have to be stepped on in numeric order. Each time a numbered spot is stepped on, its worth is added to the total. For example, when the number two spot is stepped on, it is added to the number one spot, making the team's score three million dollars. If the blindfolded person steps on a pitfall (i.e., a tennis ball), then all of his accumulated gold deposits disappear down the pitfall and the dollar amount goes to zero. The blindfolded participant and his "flashlight" cannot return back to the opening of the tunnel, but must continue from that point collecting the remaining gold deposits. For an extra challenge, blank plastic spots with no number on them can also be littered along the course to make it harder for the person that is the flashlight to discern which plastic spots are the gold deposits and which ones are fool's gold with a zero dollar value. The total amount that can possibly be collected is 55 million dollars. The team with the highest score should be recognized by the facilitator.

Preparation: The facilitator needs to set up the course by sectioning off a 15 x 15 foot square with cones, then randomly scattering 50 tennis balls, 10 plastic numbered spots, and, if desired, several blank plastic spots. Plastic spots can be purchased at a sporting goods store or paper plates can be used, with each number written in marker.

Location: Outdoors

Number of Participants: Four smaller two-person teams

Age Range: Eight and older

Discussion Points: After the game, the facilitator should ask the following questions: If you were acting as the "flashlight," what was difficult about communicating instructions to your blindfolded partner? If you were the blindfolded player, did the instructions help you avoid pitfalls while accumulating gold deposits and what could have been better in receiving instructions? What situations in your life can be represented by this game? What have you learned in this game that will help you to succeed in your life?

Safety Precautions: To avoid losing balance while walking through this course, caution should be used by the blindfolded person with each step in case he steps on a tennis ball.

Game #45: Team Tower

Objective: To create an interteam communication opportunity that should lead to sharing resources

Goals of Participants: To build the highest freestanding tower

Overview: The group is divided into three smaller teams of about five people per team. Each team is told that they need to build a tall, freestanding tower with the supplies given to them. Each team has a time limit of 25 minutes to complete its tower, and the tower should be able to stand on its own for five minutes.

Rules: The facilitator should choose his instructions carefully to create a competitive nature but not to limit the teams from combining resources to make one tall tower once they realize that cooperating and working together fulfills the objective of this game. The materials are designed to use all three supplies together in order to make the tallest tower.

Preparation: Prior to this activity the facilitator needs to assemble three paper bags (one for each team) with the following supplies: one with 50 large marshmallows, one with 100 small pretzel sticks, and one with 75 plastic straws. A stopwatch is also needed. The facilitator should let the teams combine on their own without prompting them.

Location: Indoors or outdoors

Number of Participants: Three teams of five people per team

Age Range: Eight and older

Discussion Points: After the game, the facilitator should address the need for the three teams to combine resources in order to make the tallest tower. He should then ask the following questions: At what point did the teams realize they needed to cooperate with each other? What team made the suggestion first and why? What was the final outcome and did the tower succeed in its design?

Safety Precautions: Participants should be cautioned not to eat the food materials because of sanitary reasons.

Game #46: X-Ball Scramble

Objective: To communicate and strategize with team members to discover the best methods of accomplishing a task faster than opposing teams

Goals of Participants: To accumulate points in competing with other teams

Overview: A group of 30 people is divided into 10 three-person teams with each team assigned a number from 1 to 10. Each team is responsible for retrieving a tennis ball with its team's number written on it from a five-gallon bucket that is located 20 feet away. All 10 teams share the same bucket. One person from each team races toward the bucket at the same time as the other team representatives to search and retrieve his team's ball, and then he runs back to the facilitator. The first person to reach the facilitator receives 10 points for his team, the second person receives nine points for his team, and this pattern continues until the last person to reach the facilitator receives one point for his team. The players deposit their balls into an empty bucket that is positioned next to the facilitator. Once a participant has delivered his team's ball to the facilitator, he runs back to the bucket and attempts to be the first person to retrieve and deliver the X ball, which is the remaining tennis ball and is labeled with an X on it. The first person to get that ball and bring it back receives an extra 10 points for his team. Any player that takes the X ball before he delivers his team ball receives a score of minus 50 points for his team.

Rules: Players cannot kick the ball bucket to scatter the balls or throw other balls away from the bucket. Three rounds of this game are played and a different team member is responsible for retrieving the team ball and racing after the X ball in each round. After the three rounds, the team with the most points wins the game.

Preparation: The facilitator needs 11 tennis balls, two five-gallon empty buckets, a pad of paper, a pencil, and a marker.

Location: Outdoors

Number of Participants: 10 three-person teams

Age Range: Eight and older

Discussion Points: After the game, the facilitator should ask the following questions: What strategies did team members share with each other to gain more points in each round of the game? Were the strategies modified after each round to increase the effectiveness of the team member's performance?

Safety Precautions: Participants should be cautioned not to push or shove competing team members when retrieving balls from the bucket. No physical contact should be made toward the player retrieving the X ball.

Game #47: Team Name Scramble

Objective: To build affinity among a new team

Goals of Participants: To record the time it takes for the team to unscramble its team name

Overview: After choosing their team name, the team spells out its name with paper plate letters. Each paper plate has one letter of the alphabet written on it in marker, and the plates are scattered facedown on the ground. The team sorts through the paper plates to find the necessary letters as fast as they can, using quick, decisive communication skills.

Rules: The facilitator times this event with a stopwatch. After the first round, the team plays two more rounds to improve its time by verbally organizing team members to work quickly. In addition to improving communication, the team builds unity and familiarity with their team name.

Preparation: The facilitator needs at least 60 heavy-duty paper plates (two sets of alphabet letters, plus extra plates for additional letters needed for the team name, for example, if the team name has three As in it), a stopwatch, and a marker.

Location: Outdoors on a grassy field

Number of Participants: A team of three of more

Age Range: Eight and older

Discussion Points: After the game, the facilitator should ask the following questions: Was there a leader that emerged from this game? What plan was first articulated by the leader or group of leaders to accomplish the task? Did the original plan change with additional communication for the second and third rounds of the game? How did this game bring affinity to the team?

Safety Precautions: In moving rapidly, participants should use caution not to collide with other team members in retrieving and organizing the letter plates.

5

Initiative Games

Game #48: Fly Swatter and Feather

Objective: To teach initiative in a group setting

Goals of Participants: To keep a feather from falling on the ground by using a fly swatter

Overview: The team stands in a circle and each person is given a fly swatter. Each team member works alongside other team members to keep a large feather floating in the air by only using his fly swatter. The facilitator times the group with a stopwatch to determine how long it keeps the feather in the air.

Rules: The team plays three rounds of this game, attempting to increase the length of time they are able to keep the feather off the ground.

Preparation: The facilitator needs a new fly swatter for each participant and a large turkey feather for the team. A stopwatch is also needed.

Location: Indoors

Number of Participants: A team of three to six participants

Age Range: Eight and older

Discussion Points: After the game, the facilitator should ask the following question: How did you demonstrate initiative in contributing to the team's challenge of keeping the feather in the air?

Safety Precautions: Participants should be spread out far enough to avoid getting hit by the fly swatters.

Game #49: Flying Chickens

Objective: To improve team performance in accomplishing a task

Goals of Participants: To work as a team to get as many rubber chickens through the holes of a tarp within a one-minute time frame

Overview: The team is given a tarp with five one-foot holes cut out of it and 10 rubber chickens. Each rubber chicken cannot stay on the tarp longer than three seconds and has to be flung in the air constantly until it is dropped through one of the holes in the tarp. All team members hold onto the tarp as they shake it up and down.

Rules: Each chicken that is dropped through a hole in the tarp is worth 10 points. The facilitator gives the team one minute to get as many chickens through the holes as possible. The team plays three rounds of this game, attempting to improve its score with each round.

Preparation: The facilitator needs a tarp with five one-foot holes cut out of it, 10 rubber chickens, and a stopwatch.

Location: Outdoors

Number of Participants: A team of five or more participants

Age Range: Eight and older

Discussion Points: After the game, the facilitator should ask the following question: In what ways did you show initiative in improving the overall team's performance by the third round of the game?

Safety Precautions: Team members should be spread out far enough around the tarp to prevent them from being hit by other participants as the tarp is being shaken up and down.

Game #50: Team Jump Rope

Objective: To coordinate a simultaneous team effort in performing a task

Goals of Participants: To jump in unison with team members

Overview: Two team members swing a jump rope over the heads and under the feet of at least two other team members, who attempt to jump the rope together.

Rules: A group leader should count to three and then yell, "Jump." The team members that are swinging the ropes should start off slowly and slightly increase speed during the game.

Preparation: The facilitator needs a 15-foot jump rope.

Location: Outdoors

Number of Participants: A team of four to six members

Age Range: Eight and older

Discussion Points: After the game, the facilitator should ask the following questions: What did this activity teach you about initiative? How can players take initiative and show teamwork during this game? What elements of accountability are involved in this game?

Safety Precautions: Team members should use caution when jumping to avoid tripping or being tangled up in the rope.

Game #51: Stilts Walk

Objective: To teach team members initiative in reaching out and supporting other team members as they accomplish a task

Goals of Participants: To walk through a course of hoops on stilts

Overview: A course is set up with six hoops that are laid on the ground, and, one at a time, team members walk through the course on five-foot stilts with the assistance of team members.

Rules: Team members serve as spotters, standing with their arms up near the person on stilts to give him aid and support in case he teeters or loses his balance.

Preparation: To make stilts, the facilitator needs two pieces of pine that are 1.5 x 1.5 x 60 inches long. For the footrests, he needs two pieces of oak that are 1.5 x 2.5 x 5.5 inches long. The footrests are flat on top and angled on the bottom. Each footrest is secured to a pole 12 inches from the ground with four finishing nails (two at the top of the footrest and two at the bottom). The footrests are then glued onto the stilt poles. After the glue has dried, the facilitator drills holes through the footrests and stilt poles to install two 0.25 x 5 inch carriage bolts into each pole, secured with two nuts on the other side.

Location: Outdoors

Number of Participants: A team of three to six members

Age Range: 12 and older

Discussion Points: After the game, the facilitator should ask the following question: Did you feel supported, encouraged, and safe because of the initiative and care of fellow team members?

Safety Precautions: The spotters should be alert and be prepared to steady the participant to prevent him from falling.

Game #52: Kaboom!

Objective: To develop problem solving skills

Goals of Participants: To walk along three two-by-fours as a team without spilling any water from a cup held by one team member

Overview: Before starting the game, the facilitator should set up the following scenario: The team is on a top secret mission to destroy a bridge using nitroglycerin. The team must cross three two-by-fours, which are laying end to end flat on the ground (the bridge), making sure they do not spill a drop of water (the nitroglycerin) out of a cup held by one of the team members. If they do spill, they must go back to the starting area and yell, "Kaboom," and start the process over again.

Rules: When all team members are safely on the other side of the "bridge," one person places the cup of "nitroglycerin" in the middle of the bridge. Then the team attempts to knock it over while standing six feet away, at the end of the bridge (because of the imaginary explosion that will occur when the cup is tipped over). The team should first discuss options on how they can accomplish this task from such a far distance. At the end of the team's discussion, the facilitator may suggest tying several shoes together and spinning the shoes by their laces to throw at the cup or tying several belts together and swinging them at the cup.

Preparation: The facilitator needs three two-by-fours and a paper cup filled with water.

Location: Outdoors

Number of Participants: A team of seven people

Age Range: Eight and older

Discussion Points: After the game, the facilitator should ask the following questions: Who took charge of the situation and why? Did everyone get a chance to express their ideas? How many ideas were successful in tipping the cup over and how many ideas failed? Is it okay to fail in searching for solutions?

Safety Precautions: To avoid injuries, all participants should be alert and stand out of the way when objects are being flung toward the cup of water.

Game #53: Giant's Volleyball

Objective: To teach teamwork and cooperation by using the combined strength of two groups of people to accomplish a task

Goals of Participants: To pass a large three-foot ball over a net and back

Overview: The team is divided into two smaller groups and each group stands on opposite sides of a volleyball net. The two groups attempt to pass a large three-foot exercise ball over the net, using only a twin-size flat bedsheet per group. Instead of competing with the other group, both groups work together to keep the large ball continuously moving over the net. The first group flings the ball over the net, and the second group tries to catch it in the bed sheet and pass it back to the first team.

Rules: The facilitator counts how many times the ball clears the net. Both groups focus on the same goal of reaching a high number of passes over the net. If the ball lands on the ground or goes out-of-bounds, the counting starts over.

Preparation: A large three-foot ball, two twin-size flat bedsheets, a volleyball net and stands.

Location: An outdoor volleyball court

Number of Participants: Two six-member teams

Age Range: 12 and older

Discussion Points: After the game, the facilitator should ask the following questions: What are some examples of cooperation that took place during the game? Did everyone participate in providing strength and support? How effective were the two groups in building teamwork while completing the task?

Safety Precautions: All participants should be alert and pay attention to where the ball is at all times to avoid getting hit by the ball.

Game #54: Jungle Maze

Objective: To provide an opportunity for one team member to demonstrate initiative in leading the rest of the team and for the other team members to become good followers

Goals of Participants: To lead a group through an obstacle course or to successfully follow the group leader through an obstacle course

Overview: Before starting the game, the facilitator should set up the following scenario: The team has just survived a plane crash in the dense jungle of South America in the dead of night. The captain of the plane (the group leader) only has a flashlight and must lead his passengers (the team members) through a tunnel of sharp rocks (cones) and poisonous plants (duct tape) in order to escape. The plane is on fire and will explode once the fire reaches the fuel tank, so the captain must lead everyone away from the plane as quickly as possible.

The group leader stands near the obstacle course with his eyes open. The rest of the team members crawl through the course one at a time with their eyes closed. The leader uses verbal instructions to direct each person through the course.

Rules: The leader of the team is responsible for helping each person make it through the course without touching the sticky part of the tape or the traffic cones. If a person touches either a cone or the tape, he must return to the starting area and begin again.

Preparation: The facilitator needs 12 one-and-a-half-foot tall traffic cones and a roll of duct tape. The course is created by setting up two rows of cones and draping the tape (sticky side down) across the tops of the cones, forming a "tunnel" that is 12 feet long and three feet wide with several turns in it.

Location: Indoors or outdoors

Number of Participants: A team of 10 people

Age Range: Eight and older

Discussion Points: After the game, the facilitator should assist the team as they evaluate the leader's performance in guiding everyone through the course. Then, he should ask the following questions: Was the leader clear in his instructions? Did you feel comforted by the guidance provided by the leader? Did anyone have to start over again because the directions were unclear or he did not listen to the instructions? Please explain. What suggestions could help the leader improve his leadership? How can you take initiative to be a better follower?

Safety Precautions: Participants with their eyes closed should use caution and crawl slowly through the course.

Game #55: Hammer and Nail Relay

Objective: To teach accountability and responsibility

Goals of Participants: To drive a nail into a wooden beam as fast as possible

Overview: The team runs a relay race in which each team member, one at a time, drives a nail with a hammer into a wooden beam.

Rules: The team members stand in a line five feet from a wooden beam. Each person is given a nail and has to run and hammer the nail in the beam when it is his turn. The hammer is passed from team member to team member like a baton. The team plays three rounds of this game, attempting to speed up its total time.

Preparation: The facilitator needs a two-foot long, 3.5 x 3.5 inch wooden beam, a hammer, and three-inch long nails (three per person). A stopwatch is also needed.

Location: Indoors or outdoors

Number of Participants: A team of five to eight participants

Age Range: Eight and older

Discussion Points: After the game, the facilitator should ask each team member to share his feelings about the accountability he had in performing for the team. He should then ask the following questions: Did this activity put too much pressure on you? Did you receive approval and support from others? Was there a chance to get recognition and praise after the game? What are other examples in life where you learn responsibility?

Safety Precautions: Prior to the game, instruct all participants to use extreme caution in striking the hammer so they do not accidentally strike their fingers with the hammer. Also remind them to be careful when passing the hammer to the next person and when running with the hammer and nail.

Game #56: Pencil Drop

Objective: To teach patience and persistence as each team member contributes to the overall team score

Goals of Participants: To drop a pencil into an empty two-liter soda pop bottle

Overview: The team has three minutes to drop as many pencils inside of an empty soda bottle as possible. Each team member gets three pencils and five attempts to drop a pencil into the bottle before another team member takes a turn.

Rules: The soda bottle cannot be moved from the table, and the table needs to remain on the floor during the game. Pencils should be dropped from at least one foot above the bottle.

Preparation: The facilitator needs 15 pencils, an empty two-liter soda pop bottle, and a stopwatch.

Location: Indoors

Number of Participants: A team of five participants

Age Range: Six and older

Discussion Points: After the game, the facilitator should ask the following questions: What type of leadership is required when dealing with situations that take patience and persistence? How can these situations either build a team up or break it apart? What measures can be taken by a team leader to avoid frustration, criticism, and gossip from other team members? What situations in a real-life team setting require patience and persistence?

Safety Precautions: The pencils should be unsharpened to avoid injuries.

Game #57: Straw Shapes

Objective: To provide an opportunity for participants to use creativity and dexterity in working together under pressure

Goals of Participants: To make as many shapes with bendable straws as possible in a two-minute time frame

Overview: The group is divided into smaller teams of two people per team and each pair is given five bendable straws and 12 inches of masking tape. Prior to the game, the two-person teams tape the ends of the straws together making a "straw chain." Then, the teams compete against each other to form as many shapes with the bendable straws in the two-minute time frame as they can. On each team, one person makes the shapes and the other person writes down what shapes were made. The team with the most original shapes wins the game.

Rules: The shapes only count if the straws remain taped together. Examples of shapes that can be made include: geometric shapes, letters, numbers, sports equipment, countries, states, fruits, vegetables, junk food, and constellations. Each shape must be formed by the straws and not just written down on the piece of paper.

Preparation: The facilitator needs five straws, 12 inches of masking tape, a piece of paper, and a pencil for each team. A stopwatch is also needed.

Location: Indoors

Number of Participants: Several two-person teams

Age Range: Eight and older

Discussion Points: After the game, the facilitator should ask the following questions: In what ways were you nimble and creative in coming up with different shapes? What kinds of personal experiences (e.g., geometry class, family vacation, favorite hobby) did you draw from to create additional shapes?

Safety Precautions: Participants should use caution in handling the straws to avoid eye injuries.

6

Tenacity Games

Game #58: Rapid-Fire

Objective: To teach endurance in a fast-paced game that requires perseverance and determination in order to succeed

Goals of Participants: To keep 10 balls in constant motion

Overview: A larger team is divided into smaller groups that compete with each other for the best time. Each group of six people stands in a circle and faces each other. One person in each group is selected to start throwing tennis balls to the other players in the circle (up to 10 balls total). The tennis balls have to be in constant motion from one person to another once the game has started. The purpose of the game is to keep as many balls as possible in motion for 10 minutes.

Rules: No one can hold a ball for longer than one second. Any time a ball is dropped, it is *not* retrieved. However, the group will be deducted one minute of the 10-minute time frame for each dropped ball. The team with the highest time wins the game. All balls should be thrown softly underhand.

Preparation: The facilitator needs 10 tennis balls for each group and one stopwatch.

Location: Outdoors

Number of Participants: At least two groups of six people

Age Range: Eight and older

Discussion Points: After the game, the facilitator should ask the following questions: What methods were used to persevere and succeed in the game? In a game that required constant attention, how did each team member cope with trying to juggle multiple balls? What type of leadership could have helped in balancing the balls? What are examples in life where balance is important in juggling many things at the same time? What is a lesson learned in this game that will help you maintain more balance in your life?

Safety Precautions: To avoid getting hit by a ball, each participant should be alert and aware of where the balls are at all times.

Game #59: Seven Bananas

Objective: To teach participants to endure and carry on in a positive manner despite opposition and hardship

Goals of Participants: To act quickly and avoid getting sprayed by water

Overview: The team stands in a circle facing each other, and the facilitator stands in the middle of the circle facing the players with a squirt bottle. Seven of the participants are assigned a banana number (one through seven). The other three participants are assigned the names *what*, *who*, and *how many,* and only the facilitator, who is assigned the name *monkey*, can call on these people. To avoid being squirted by the facilitator, a person needs to call out another person's banana number or yell "Monkey" as quickly as possible when his number is called.

Rules: The facilitator cannot call on any of the banana numbers. Instead, he must call on *what*, *who*, or *how many*. For example, if the person that is *two bananas* says, "Monkey" and the facilitator says, "How many," the person that is *how many* quickly replies, "Six bananas," and the game continues when the person that is *six bananas* calls a different banana number or the word *monkey*. If everyone responds quickly, then no one gets squirted by the spray bottle. If the facilitator delays in his response longer than three seconds, he has to trade places with the person that is *one banana*.

Preparation: A spray bottle with a yellow piece of paper with a picture of a banana on it taped to the bottle.

Location: Outdoors

Number of Participants: A team of 10 people

Age Range: 12 and older

Discussion Points: After the game, the facilitator should ask the following questions: Despite getting sprayed with water or feeling pressure to respond quickly, how were you able to maintain a positive attitude when your name was called? What methods did you use to not become discouraged? How can these same methods be used in real-life situations during a hardship or trial?

Safety Precautions: If any participant is continually being sprayed, the facilitator should check with him to ensure that he is still enjoying the game and is not becoming too discouraged and wants to quit.

Game #60: Leaky Garbage Can

Objective: To solve a problem as a team by having certain team members sacrifice personal comfort so the rest of the team can succeed

Goals of Participants: To maintain a high water level in a garbage can that has several holes in it

Overview: The team is given the task of filling up a garbage can that has holes in it with water by putting some team members in the garbage can to plug the holes from the inside, while others plug the holes from the outside of the can. Still other team members fill up gallon-size buckets of water to fill up the garbage can.

Rules: The team has a three-minute time limit to attempt to fill up the leaky garbage can to its brim.

Preparation: The facilitator needs three clean plastic garbage cans (two 10-gallon cans with no holes and one 20-gallon can with 30 dime-size holes along the sides of the container). The cans with no holes are filled to the top with water from a garden hose, and these containers are what team members use to fill up the buckets to transfer to the leaky garbage can. The team should have six gallon-size buckets. The facilitator also needs a stopwatch.

Location: Outdoors in a grassy field

Number of Participants: A team of 10 people

Age Range: Eight and older

Discussion Points: After the game, the facilitator should ask the following questions: How did it feel to sit in the garbage can during the game while cold water was being dumped around you? Did you feel appreciated for the inconvenience you experienced? What other important leadership roles were developed during this game? Do you feel like you succeeded as a team in this game? Why?

Safety Precautions: The grassy area will become slippery from the water and participants should use caution to prevent themselves from falling while running back and forth between the garbage cans.

Game #61: Dented Tin Can

Objective: To teach leadership in developing team members' full potential

Goals of Participants: To play the game Kick the Can with a #10 tin can and then use that can as a flower pot

Overview: The team plays the game Kick the Can. By the end of the game, the can will be dented and kicked in, which seems to leave it without much use except for scrap. However, the team will transform it into something useful again by planting several beautiful flowers in it. The facilitator will explain that a leader should not give up on a fellow team member too soon without developing that person's full potential—like the tin can that was kicked around in one activity and in another activity was used to hold items of beauty. A leader has the responsibility to find a purpose and a meaningful role and responsibility for each of his team members and then watch each person grow and develop into that role.

Rules: One person is "it" and counts to 50 while everyone else hides. The person that is "it" seeks to find the hidden players and identify who they are. The person that is "it" must then race back to the can and call out the person's name that he identified. If the person that was hiding can reach the can and kick it over before the person that is "it" does, then that person is safe and can continue playing. If the person that is "it" reaches the can first and says the person's name, then that person is out of the game. Play continues until everyone is out of the game.

Preparation: A facilitator needs an empty #10 tin can and some potting soil and flowers.

Location: Outdoors

Number of Participants: A team of 5 to 10 people

Age Range: Eight and older

Discussion Points: After the game, the facilitator should ask the following questions: How did the game Kick the Can represent some people's negative self-image of themselves? What does the old adage "Don't judge a book by its cover" mean? What are some ways not to judge other people too hastily? What value was set on the can once the flowers were inside? What lesson of inner beauty can be taught from this activity? As leaders, what are action steps that we can take to help team members reach their full potential?

Safety Precautions: To avoid injuries, the empty tin can should be free of jagged edges.

Game #62: Yo-Yo Spin

Objective: To teach determination and stamina

Goals of Participants: To work together to knock racquetballs off of cones using only a hoop and two yo-yos

Overview: The group is divided into smaller teams of two people. Each pair stands inside a hoop with two yo-yos affixed to the hoop with tape (spaced an equal distance apart on the hoop). The team then attempts to knock racquetballs off of cones that are placed behind the participants by swinging the hoop around while standing stationary.

Rules: Only the yo-yos can touch the racquetballs on the cones. The two people can work together in trying to knock off one racquetball at a time, which requires them to use focus and coordinate swinging the hoop in one direction.

Preparation: The facilitator needs two three-foot cones, two racquetballs, one hoop, two yo-yos, and masking tape.

Location: Indoors or outdoors

Number of Participants: Several two-person teams

Age Range: Eight and older

Discussion Points: After the game, the facilitator should ask the following questions: Was this an easy task? If not, what was difficult about it? What lessons in patience and determination can be learned by solving the problem? How can resilience and fortitude help us accomplish difficult things in our life?

Safety Precautions: The hoop should not be swung too fast so the yo-yos hit the team members in the leg.

Game #63: Flying Saucers

Objective: To teach resiliency and patience as participants must work against the clock to accomplish a difficult task

Goals of Participants: To work as a team to throw balls into a bucket while being timed

Overview: The team works together to throw specially-designed balls into a bucket that is held by a fellow team member. Six soft, foam balls are attached to each other with string and cloth webbing. When participants throw the balls, they spin through the air like a flying saucer.

Rules: Approximately 10 feet away from the team is a team member that holds a large bucket on his head and acts as the catcher—moving from side to side but not front to back—as he attempts to catch the flying balls (saucers). Any ball that misses the bucket has to be retrieved and thrown again. The facilitator times the group to see how long it takes the team to accomplish the task of getting five "flying saucers" in the bucket. All of the balls must be in the bucket for the time to stop. The team plays three rounds of this game, attempting to improve its speed with each round.

Preparation: To make a "flying saucer," the facilitator stitches yarn with a large needle to a 6 x 6-inch piece of tulle, attaching the six soft, foam balls along the edges of the tulle. The six attached flying saucer balls can also be commercially purchased. In addition to five flying saucers, the facilitator also needs a large bucket and a stopwatch.

Location: Outdoors

Number of Participants: A team of 5 to 10 players

Age Range: Eight and older

Discussion Points: After the game, the facilitator should ask the following questions: What lessons did you learn by constantly having to rethrow missed balls toward the bucket? Did the catcher feel limited in his efforts to catch the ball because he could only move from side to side? Did the team feel successful after they had persisted in performing three rounds of the game? Did the last round of the game have the best time?

Safety Precautions: All participants should be alert to the flying balls around them to avoid getting hit by the balls.

Game #64: Team Ball

Objective: To teach determination and resolve in completing a task with another person

Goals of Participants: To complete a course in the shortest amount of time with another team member while holding a plunger and ball

Overview: A group is divided into smaller teams of two people, and each pair has to pick up a five-inch playground ball off the ground using plungers and carry the ball 25 feet while weaving in and out of cones.

Rules: Only the plungers can touch the ball as it is picked up and carried to the finish line. Each team is timed and the team that accomplishes the job the fastest wins the game. If the team drops the ball before reaching the finish line, then the team must go back to the starting area and begin again.

Preparation: The facilitator needs a plunger for each participant and a five-inch playground ball for each team. A stopwatch is also needed for the game.

Location: Outdoors

Number of Participants: At least four two-person teams

Age Range: Eight and older

Discussion Points: After the game, the facilitator should ask the following questions: (To the winning team) Did sheer determination and willpower help you accomplish the job in the fastest time? (To the other teams) Was determination and drive to succeed a part the game plan? Did determination and the desire to win the game unite you as a team or cause tension and division among you and your partner? If there was tension, what other goal or outcome would have helped your team to become more unified?

Safety Precautions: The plungers should be new and unused for any plumbing maintenance so they are sanitary and safe.

Game #65: Tennis Ball Slide

Objective: To provide an opportunity to demonstrate that a mundane task can be used to promote positive morale for the entire team

Goals of Participants: To form a line holding two-foot-long pieces of two-inch-wide PVC pipes and roll tennis balls down the pipes toward a crate at the end of the line

Overview: Before the game, the facilitator sets up the scenario that the tennis balls are explosive cannons and cannot be dropped. When a ball is dropped, the team must run 10 feet away and yell, "Bang" three times. Then, the team must start over by taking all of the tennis balls out of the crate and bringing them back to the starting area.

Rules: The PVC pipes cannot touch each other as players make the line. The facilitator starts the balls rolling at one end. He starts out slowly and increases the rate at which the balls are put on the pipe toward the end of the game. The facilitator can also send multiple balls down the pipe at the same time.

Preparation: The facilitator needs a two-foot-long by two-inch-wide piece of PVC pipe for each player, 25 tennis balls, and a crate.

Location: Outdoors

Number of Participants: A group of 10 people

Age Range: Eight and older

Discussion Points: After the game, the facilitator should ask the following questions: Was a leader appointed for the group or did a leader emerge as the game was getting organized? Did the leader help lead the team with a positive attitude despite setbacks and discouragement? Was the team's morale impacted by the leader's attitude toward starting the game again after a ball was dropped? What could each player do to keep a positive attitude and influence other team members to do the same?

Safety Precautions: When a ball is dropped and the team scrambles to yell, "Bang," participants should watch for tennis balls on the ground to prevent from tripping over them.

Game #66: Mini-Triathlon

Objective: To provide an opportunity for teammates to encourage and support each other during an activity that requires major physical exertion and determination

Goals of Participants: To bike six miles, run a mile and a half, and swim four laps in an Olympic-size pool as a team

Overview: The focus for this mini-triathlon is not to see who gets the fastest time, but to start at the same time and finish as a team.

Rules: One suggestion on coordinating the course is to bike to a nearby community recreation center that totals six miles or more roundtrip. Then, the team runs the mile and a half either at an indoor track at the recreation center or in a nearby neighborhood and returns back to the center to swim the four laps in the swimming pool.

Preparation: Each team member needs a bike helmet, a bike with a lock, athletic clothing, running shoes, a swimsuit, and a towel. The facilitator should have water available for team members to drink at each station.

Location: A community recreation center or a public school facility with a swimming pool

Number of Participants: A team of five participants

Age Range: 12 and older

Discussion Points: After the game, the facilitator should ask the following questions: What was difficult about this activity? What was easy about it? Was enduring the hardship of this activity made easier by the camaraderie of the team as you worked through it together? What would it be like to attempt this mini-triathlon alone, without your team? What type of team unity occurred as a result of this activity?

Safety Precautions: Participants should follow all traffic laws and recreation center rules when participating in this mini-triathlon. The facilitator should inspect all bikes to ensure that they are in working order. A bicycle repair kit should be packed for the trip as well. Any participant with a medical condition that would be impacted by this activity should seek the approval of his physician prior to the event.

7

Goal Setting Games

Game #67: Wooden Squares Switch

Objective: To set a goal and work together to achieve that goal

Goals of Participants: To exchange places with another group while standing on wooden squares

Overview: The team stands on wooden squares in a half circle formation, with an open square at the center dividing the team into two groups. The participants must move from one side of the half circle to the other by switching places with adjacent members of the other group, until the two groups have completely switched sides.

Rules: The game begins with the two players at the front of each group (i.e., on either side of the open center square) switching places with each other. Then, those two players continue switching places with adjacent members of the other group until they are at the front of their group again, on the opposite side. All the other players do the same, switching places with adjacent members of the other group to move forward to the square next to the open center square, so they can move to the other side and then advance to their original positions in their group. Switches must take place one at a time on alternating sides of the half circle. Participants can only go forward and not backward. Once a participant has switched to the other side, he cannot stand next to another player from his group until he has reached his final position. The open square should always be at the center of the half circle. If any of the rules are broken, the game starts over. A hint to make this game easier is to have all the players stand in their direction of travel to make it clear which group each person belongs to.

Preparation: The facilitator needs 11 two-foot squares made of plywood.

Location: Outdoors or indoors

Number of Participants: Two groups of five players

Age Range: 12 and older

Discussion Points: After the game, the facilitator should ask the following questions: Was there any point during the game that you felt you could not obtain the goal and why? What were some steps that were taken in advancing toward the goal? How is the rule of not being able to go backward without starting the game over symbolic in goal setting?

Safety Precautions: When moving to a square, each participant can step off of his current square onto the ground and then step back onto the next square without having to hop or jump to that square.

Game #68: Rope Shapes

Objective: To teach the importance of having vision as a leader when working toward a goal

Goals of Participants: To make different shapes with a large rope

Overview: Team members stand in a circle and hold onto a rope with their eyes closed. One team member is the leader and he stands outside of the circle with his eyes open, but he cannot talk. The rest of the team can talk with each other as they are silently directed by the leader as he gently moves them by the shoulders into positions to make different formations.

Rules: The facilitator gives the team leader a list of the following shapes to make: a square, a triangle, a hexagon, and a five-pointed star.

Preparation: The facilitator needs a long 25-foot rope for this activity.

Location: Outdoors

Number of Participants: 10 players

Age Range: Eight and older

Discussion Points: After the game, the facilitator should ask the following questions: Do you feel that the leader had the necessary vision to lead the group in accomplishing the final goal? Did other team members feel like they could give input or ask questions to the leader? What situations in a real-life setting would resemble the scenario that the leader needs to see the final goal in order help others? In this situation, how could followers still be able to ask questions and contribute solutions to reaching the goal?

Safety Precautions: Participants with their eyes closed should use caution when walking to avoid stumbling. The playing area should be free of low hanging branches or tripping hazards.

Game #69: Flip the Tarp

Objective: To achieve a goal as a team despite obstacles and hardships

Goals of Participants: To flip a tarp over while standing on it

Overview: The team is given a 4 x 4-foot tarp for everyone to stand on, and they have to flip it completely over while still standing on it.

Rules: No one is allowed to step off the tarp as it is being flipped over and if they do, the team must start the game over. A hint to completing this task is to fold the tarp up into smaller triangles where no one is standing, then twist that section over and move the team into the new section and fold up the other section as the team moves over.

Preparation: The facilitator needs a 4 x 4-foot tarp for this activity.

Location: Outdoors

Number of Participants: A team of 10 participants

Age Range: Eight and older

Discussion Points: After the game, the facilitator should ask the following questions: Did you think this task was possible when you first started the activity? Did your team try all of the ideas suggested by team members? What suggestions worked best? In obtaining goals, how important is it to consider all suggested ideas before beginning? What is the best way to get ideas to achieve goals? What are examples that team members have faced with obstacles that they encountered when achieving a goal?

Safety Precautions: Participants should not sit on the shoulders of fellow team members to play this game.

Game #70: Frisbee Challenge

Objective: To illustrate the importance of aiming toward goals and persisting in reaching them

Goals of Participants: To take turns tossing a Frisbee toward various goals (targets) that are scattered around a playing area

Overview: This game is a team version of Frisbee golf with one accumulative score. The goals are different objects to be thrown in, at, or through. Each person keeps track of his throws to add to the team's overall score.

Rules: Players on the team take turns in getting the Frisbee to the designated goal. Two traffic cones mark the starting line for the first goal, and each goal acts as the starting line for the next goal, i.e., goal #1 is the starting line for goal #2, and so on. If the goal is missed on the first attempt, the player picks up the Frisbee where it landed and throws it from there, adding each throw to his score. The course is a nine-hole course with the following goals:

1. To land the Frisbee in a hoop that is lying on the ground six feet away
2. To fling the Frisbee and knock down three paper cups that are in a pyramid formation on a chair eight feet away

3. To land the Frisbee inside a large bucket eight feet away
4. To land the Frisbee between two traffic cones that are 15 feet away
5. To "shoot" the Frisbee through a basketball net from the free-throw line
6. To throw the Frisbee over an eight-foot ladder from a distance of five feet
7. To land the Frisbee within six inches of a water balloon that is on a paper plate without breaking the water balloon. If the water balloon breaks, the team adds an extra 50 "throws" to its score. The Frisbee is thrown from a distance of five feet.
8. To throw the Frisbee over the head of a person who is standing eight feet away, trying to swat the Frisbee down with a tennis racket
9. To throw the Frisbee through a vertical hoop held chest-high by the facilitator, who is standing 10 feet away

Preparation: The facilitator needs a Frisbee, four traffic cones, a water balloon, a paper plate, a large bucket, a ladder, two hoops, one chair, one tennis racket, and three paper cups for this game.

Location: Outdoors near a basketball court

Number of Participants: A team of nine players

Age Range: Eight and older

Discussion Points: After the game, the facilitator should ask the following questions: How was each goal that you aimed for different? Were the goals difficult or easy to reach? Are all goals in life individually tailored to fit each person? Do they vary in difficulty? Why?

Safety Precautions: Participants should watch where the Frisbee is at all times to avoid getting hit.

Game #71: Wild West Shooting Gallery

Objective: To balance speed with accuracy in obtaining goals

Goals of Participants: To take turns performing two tasks as quickly as possible in relay fashion

Overview: One at a time, each team member "rides a horse" (i.e., bounces on a large exercise ball) to the shooting range where he attempts to hit plastic cups with foam darts using a toy gun in the shortest amount of time. While shooting the dart gun, each participant lies on his stomach and aims toward the target. When 10 darts are fired, the player climbs back on his "horse" and rides back to the team where another team member takes his turn.

Rules: The targets are eight feet away from the participant, and for every cup that is hit, the team receives 10 points. The team is timed from the first participant to the last participant to see how long it takes the entire team to complete these two tasks. For every 10 points earned, the team is allowed to take 20 seconds off its total time. The facilitator should keep score.

Preparation: The facilitator needs a dart gun with foam darts, disposable plastic cups, a large exercise ball, cones, a stopwatch, a pencil, and a pad of paper.

Location: Outdoors

Number of Participants: A team of five participants

Age Range: 12 and older

Discussion Points: After the game, the facilitator should ask the following questions: How did you balance racing toward the shooting range with focusing and aiming at the targets? In a real-life team setting, what are examples where speed and accuracy need to be in balance to reach goals?

Safety Precautions: Traffic cones should section off the shooting range and all participants should be behind the shooting range.

Game #72: Harmony

Objective: To emphasize that one of the most important goals as a team is harmony

Goals of Participants: To work together in playing music with handbells

Overview: Each person on the team is given a handbell and they play music together.

Rules: One way to play handbells is to use sheet music, which would require everyone to have the ability to read music. Another way is to convert the musical notes into different colors and mark the colors in two-inch circles on a poster board. Most handbells for children are color coded with the musical notes they represent (e.g., blue = A, purple = B, red = C, orange = D, yellow = E, green = F, and light blue = G). So the facilitator, for example, would point to the light blue circle for the musical note G, and all of the participants who are holding light blue handbells would ring them at that time. For this activity, the process of learning the song is more important than being able to play the song really well.

Preparation: The facilitator needs a handbell for each participant and a color-coded poster to conduct from.

Location: Indoors or outdoors

Number of Participants: A group of seven people or more

Age Range: Eight and older

Discussion Points: After the game, the facilitator should ask the following questions: What lessons in working together and in goal setting did you learn from this game? What elements of personal accountability were illustrated with this activity? What does it mean to be in harmony or in sync with each other?

Safety Precautions: Team members should be aware of participants with sensitive hearing and should not play too closely to them or too loudly near them.

Game #73: Popcorn Quest

Objective: To teach the importance of delegating and how it impacts goal setting

Goals of Participants: To build a fire and cook popcorn in the least amount of time

Overview: A leader is selected on the team and his goal is to give assignments to team members to build a fire and cook popcorn while being timed by the facilitator.

Rules: The fire should be started in a designated fire pit. Only one kernel needs to pop for the stopwatch to stop.

Preparation: The facilitator needs five matches, a small amount of tinder, 10 pieces of kindling, five small logs, six pieces of popcorn, a teaspoon of oil, a small cooking pot, a container of water to put out the fire, and a stopwatch.

Location: Outdoors

Number of Participants: A team of five participants

Age Range: 12 and older

Discussion Points: After the game, the facilitator should ask the following questions: How effective was the delegation of assignments in reaching the overall goal? What are other examples in a real-life team setting where delegating would help the team obtain its goal?

Safety Precautions: To avoid burns and other injuries, participants should use extra care and caution when building the fire and cooking the popcorn even though the team is being timed for speed.

Game #74: Puzzle Relay

Objective: To work toward a common goal without verbal communication and direction

Goals of Participants: To complete a 24-piece puzzle in the shortest amount of time

Overview: The team is divided into two smaller groups that compete against each other to put together a puzzle in the least amount of time. Members of the group have to accomplish this goal without talking to each other or to the other group.

Rules: Both groups start at the same time and the group that finishes first should raise their hands in the air and yell, "Done!"

Preparation: Two 24-piece puzzles with large pieces and two tables are needed by the facilitator. The puzzle pieces are scrambled up with the picture side facing down by the facilitator prior to the game.

Location: Indoors or outdoors

Number of Participants: A team of 12 people divided into two smaller groups

Age Range: Eight and older

Discussion Points: After the game, the facilitator should ask the following questions: What are examples of common goals that need little to no direction and communication? (Such examples may include a study group or a work team where each member fulfills his responsibility and assignments without reminders or discussion.) In achieving these types of goals, how do you know what part to play and how do you carry out your roles without direction? In these types of situations, who is responsible in providing correction or praise for individual assignments that impact the whole team? Is this type of communication a form of leadership?

Safety Precautions: Team members should use caution in moving quickly to avoid injuries to themselves or other team members.

Game #75: Ball Sort

Objective: To set goals to improve performance

Goals of Participants: To sort different kinds of balls into separate buckets as quickly as possible

Overview: A garbage can holding 200 assorted balls is dumped out onto the grass by the facilitator and team members sort the balls by type and place them in separate buckets.

Rules: This event is timed to see how the team organizes itself to accomplish the task. Three rounds of this game are played in an attempt to enhance team performance by setting specific goals to improve.

Preparation: The facilitator needs a clean, empty garbage can, 200 assorted balls (e.g., tennis balls, golf balls, racquetballs, foosballs, and small plastic balls), five clean three-gallon buckets, and a stopwatch.

Location: Outdoors on a grassy field

Number of Participants: A team of 10 players

Age Range: Six and older

Discussion Points: After the game, the facilitator should ask the following questions: What goals did you make at the beginning of the game? What goals did you make on the second and third rounds of the game to improve performance? How did the goals change from the first part of the game to the last?

Safety Precautions: Team members should use caution in moving quickly to avoid injuries to themselves or other team members.

Game #76: Flour Ball

Objective: To be on "target" with goal setting, meaning to have benchmarks to monitor progress and development

Goals of Participants: To throw stockings full of flour toward a large target

Overview: Team members take turns throwing balls of flour at an archery target that is 25 feet away. When a ball hits the target, it will leave a powdery mark. The team attempts to score 100 points with 15 throws.

Rules: Each person gets three attempts to hit the target. On the face of the target is a bull's-eye scoring system consisting of 10 circles with each circle having a number from one to 10 in value. The center circle is worth 10 points.

Preparation: The facilitator needs three cups of all-purpose wheat flour, three nylon stockings, three rubber bands, and a bull's-eye target. Prior to the game, the facilitator should fill the nylon stockings with the flour, and secure them with the rubber bands.

Location: Outdoors

Number of Participants: A team of five players

Age Range: Eight and older

Discussion Points: After the game, the facilitator should ask the following questions: How does scoring on the target symbolize benchmarks or "report cards" in goal setting? What are real benchmarks or measuring tools in a team setting that can help chart progress toward goals?

Safety Precautions: Because of possible gluten allergies, the flour balls should only be thrown toward the target and not toward other team members. Also, each participant should wash his hands after playing this game.

Game #77: Big Ball Boccie

Objective: To rely on the collective strength of the team in order to aim for the goal

Goals of Participants: To compete with each other in throwing a large exercise ball as close to a tennis ball as possible

Overview: To begin the game, a tennis ball is rolled onto the grass, and then each team rolls its large exercise ball to determine which team comes closest to the tennis ball without actually touching it.

Rules: The unique element about this game is that all team members need to be touching the exercise ball as the team rolls it toward the tennis ball. Unlike traditional boccie, where a player has four small balls to throw toward the target, each team has one ball and four chances to throw it toward the target (the tennis ball). One point is awarded to the team that can get its ball closest to the tennis ball. Several rounds of the game are played until one team reaches nine points.

Preparation: The facilitator needs three large exercise balls and a tennis ball.

Location: Outdoors

Number of Participants: Three teams of three players per team

Age Range: Eight and older

Discussion Points: After the game, the facilitator should ask the following questions: How did the collective efforts among teammates help in reaching the goal? In addition to providing strength and support, how did team members communicate with each other to accomplish the goal?

Safety Precautions: Participants on other teams should be spaced out during the game to avoid getting hit by one of the exercise balls.

8

Adaptability Games

Game #78: One-Minute Constellations

Objective: To teach adaptability to changing circumstances

Goals of Participants: To make as many constellation models as possible in a one-minute time frame

Overview: The team is given a box of toothpicks and a bag of mini-marshmallows and is timed to see how many constellation models they can make using those supplies in one minute.

Rules: The team is allowed a one-minute planning meeting and is then given one minute to perform the task. Different constellations should be assigned to different team members during the planning meeting. At the meeting, team members are allowed to talk. In the construction phase of the constellation models, team members must remain silent until the end of the one-minute task. A constellation field guide can only be referred to during the one-minute planning meeting. At the end of the game, team members exchange their constellations. Each team member can now speak and he tries to interpret and explain what the name of someone else's constellation is and where it belongs in the night sky to the facilitator without the use of the field guide.

Preparation: The facilitator needs a box of toothpicks, a bag of mini-marshmallows, and a stopwatch.

Location: Indoors or outdoors

Number of Participants: A team of five people

Age Range: Eight and older

Discussion Points: After the game, the facilitator should ask the following questions: How did you adapt to the different rules of the game? How did you "think on your feet" during the last phase of the game when you had to interpret a constellation model made by another participant?

Safety Precautions: Participants should use caution in handling the sharp toothpicks to avoid injuries.

Game #79: Blindfolded Hockey Stick Walk

Objective: To accomplish a task that requires all participants to be flexible and teachable in order to succeed

Goals of Participants: To walk through cones blindfolded while supporting a large exercise ball using only hockey sticks

Overview: The team works together to navigate through a course of traffic cones blindfolded. Each team member is holding a hockey stick and they collectively try to balance a large exercise ball on all of the sticks.

Rules: Prior to the game, a leader is selected by the team and he is not blindfolded, rather he guides the team verbally. If the ball is dropped or a member of the team is no longer touching the exercise ball, then the team must go back and start from the beginning.

Preparation: The facilitator needs a hockey stick and a blindfold for each team member. A large exercise ball and six traffic cones are also needed for this game.

Location: Outdoors

Number of Participants: A team of five participants

Age Range: Eight and older

Discussion Points: After the game, the facilitator should ask the following questions: How did you rely on the support of team members and the guidance of the team leader to accomplish this task? Did this exercise require flexibility? How? Give an example of how you were teachable during this game.

Safety Precautions: The hockey sticks should be held up at least a foot off the ground to prevent the blindfolded team members from tripping over them. The team moves slowly and cautiously during the course. The team leader and the facilitator should act as spotters as needed throughout the game.

Game #80: Water Balloon Parachute

Objective: To teach the importance of being resilient and flexible in a team setting

Goals of Participants: To makes a parachute so that two water balloons can sustain a 10-foot fall

Overview: The team has 15 minutes to make a parachute out of a plastic shopping bag and 12 inches of masking tape and then to secure the parachute to two water balloons. After the 15 minute prep time, the team drops the parachute from a height of 10 feet.

Rules: The team can only use the shopping bag and masking tape to make the parachute for the water balloons. The balloons are filled halfway with water. If the balloons sustain the first fall, then the team can attempt a drop from a height of 15 or 20 feet.

Preparation: The facilitator needs one shopping bag, two water balloons, and 12 inches of masking tape.

Location: Outdoors

Number of Participants: A team of 5 to 10 people

Age Range: Eight and older

Discussion Points: After the game, the facilitator should ask the following questions: What lesson did you learn about resiliency? As a leader, how can leading with flexibility help the team accomplish any task?

Safety Precautions: The platform where the parachute is launched needs to be a safe setting for the team such as a bridge, deck, or balcony with a railing. Prior to this activity, the facilitator should contact the property owner, the school principal, or the camp director to seek permission to drop the parachute and to make him aware that this is an organized activity—not an unsupervised water fight. No one should be directly below the drop site where they might get hit by the water balloons.

Game #81: String Ball

Objective: To demonstrate that in team relationships, give-and-take by leaders and team members is necessary at times to keep morale high and rapport strong among the team

Goals of Participants: To work as a team to maneuver a ball on a web of string for the longest amount of time

Overview: The team sits on the ground in a circle. One person takes a ball of string and holds the end of the string, then tosses the ball to another person on the other side of the circle. That person holds onto his section of string and tosses the ball to another person in a different section of the circle. This pattern continues until the string is crisscrossing through the center of the circle, forming a web. Once the string is taut enough to support a volleyball, the facilitator begins timing with the stopwatch. The team must keep the ball in continual movement and the goal is to go at least 10 or 15 minutes without stopping.

Rules: If the ball gets tangled in the string, the team must untangle it by moving the strings up and down in an attempt to dislodge the ball. If a person touches the ball, if the ball falls on the ground, or if the ball is tangled in the string for longer than one minute, the facilitator stops the stopwatch and the team starts the game over.

Preparation: The facilitator needs 50 yards of string, a volleyball, and a stopwatch.

Location: Outdoors

Number of Participants: A team of 20 people

Age Range: Eight and older

Discussion Points: After the game, the facilitator should ask the following questions: What are examples of give-and-take situations in a real team setting? How can collaboration among team members help maintain healthy and productive relationships? How can the team leader be instrumental in initiating this kind of collaboration?

Safety Precautions: All participants should be aware of where the ball is at all times to avoid being hit with the ball during the game.

Game #82: Blindfolded Ping-Pong Ball Walk

Objective: To increase agility, dexterity, and balance in performing a difficult task

Goals of Participants: To lead a blindfolded partner through an obstacle course

Overview: The participant that is blindfolded must walk through an obstacle course with a Ping-Pong ball on a spoon in his mouth. His partner leads him through the course with verbal guidance and also serves as a spotter to help him with balance and control. The course is set up with chairs that the blindfolded person must weave around to get to the finish line. When he gets to the end, he tries to drop the ball into a bucket that is on the floor.

Rules: If the Ping-Pong ball falls off the spoon during the course, the blindfolded player must go back to the starting line and restart the course. When the blindfolded person tries to drop the ball into the bucket at the end of the course, he does not need to start over if he misses the bucket. When the blindfolded player finishes the course, he trades places with his partner and they go through the course again.

Preparation: The facilitator will need two plastic spoons, one blindfold, and a Ping-Pong ball for each team. One bucket and several chairs for the obstacles are also needed.

Location: Indoors or outdoors

Number of Participants: Four teams of two people per team

Age Range: Eight and older

Discussion Points: After the game, the facilitator should ask the following questions: While blindfolded, how did you maintain balance and poise while going through the obstacle course? What are examples of real-life situations in a team setting that are like this game, where balance, nimbleness, and grace are needed in an ever-changing environment?

Safety Precautions: The blindfolded participant should walk slowly with the spoon in his mouth. Any tripping hazards or obstructions (aside from the chairs, which serve as the obstacles) should be removed from the course. The player who serves as the guide should assist with careful verbal guidance to prevent his partner from stumbling.

Game #83: Shoes

Objective: To teach the importance of being flexible and adaptable in organizing a team

Goals of Participants: To organize themselves by shoe style and size while holding hands

Overview: The team forms a circle and holds hands while standing up. Then, without breaking the handclasps, the group organizes itself based on shoe color, standing in order from the person with the lightest colored pair to the person with the darkest color. In the next round of the game, without breaking the handclasps, the team organizes itself based on shoe size, standing in order from the smallest size to the biggest size.

Rules: The handclasps cannot be broken; however, the handclasps can be rotated around a team member's wrists to prevent his hands or arms from being twisted and bent. Participants must remain standing during the entire game.

Preparation: The facilitator needs a large, open area.

Location: Indoors or outdoors

Number of Participants: A team of 15 members

Age Range: Eight and older

Discussion Points: After the game, the facilitator should ask the following question: How was being flexible physically in this activity symbolic of being flexible in a real team setting when trying to get organized?

Safety Precautions: The facilitator can stop the game for handclasps to be adjusted to increase comfort anytime during the activity.

Game #84: Unified

Objective: To promote team spirit

Goals of Participants: To connect the team together with yarn

Overview: The team stands in a line and strings one piece of yarn through each participant's shirt to connect everyone.

Rules: The first player should run the yarn in through his left sleeve and out of his back collar, then drape it outside the shirt, down the back of his right shoulder. Then, the string is passed to the next participant in line and he follows the same pattern. This pattern continues until everyone is connected to each other.

Preparation: The facilitator needs a ball of yarn.

Location: Indoors or outdoors

Number of Participants: A team of 10 people

Age Range: Eight and older

Discussion Points: After the game, the facilitator should explain how the team was unified by a common thread and then ask for examples of other "common threads" that unify the team's spirit such as common hobbies and goals.

Safety Precautions: The yarn should be moved slowly so that no one gets a rope burn on the back of his neck. To prevent discomfort, any participant with sunburns, rashes, or open sores on their shoulders, back, or neck should not participate in this activity.

Game #85: Island Crossing

Objective: To illustrate the importance of mobilizing a group through well-thought-out but adaptable plans

Goals of Participants: To walk across a human bridge

Overview: Before starting the game, the facilitator should set up the following scenario: A volcano has erupted and all of the island inhabitants have to cross a large lagoon on a "human bridge" toward another island. The six people that make up the bridge are standing on a slippery coral reef in the lagoon and the inhabitants must constantly hold onto the human bridge or they will fall into the lagoon.

Rules: The human bridge is made up of individual team members who hold hands and stand with their feet placed inside the two holes of cinder blocks that are spaced three feet away from each other. The island inhabitants are team members who cross the bridge by walking along the tops of the cinder blocks, maintaining constant contact by touching the arms or shoulders of the people forming the bridge. If a player falls off or loses contact with a member of the bridge, then that person must start over again.

Preparation: The facilitator needs six cinder blocks and a large playing area.

Location: Outdoors

Number of Participants: A team of 12 players (Six players make up the human bridge, and six players are the island inhabitants.)

Age Range: 12 and older

Discussion Points: After the game, the facilitator should ask the following questions: What lessons did you learn about mobilizing a group quickly and effectively in this mock emergency? What did you learn about the value of being adaptable to changing situations?

Safety Precautions: All participants should wear closed-toe shoes and use caution in climbing on and off the cinder blocks.

9

Affinity Games

Game #86: United Values

Objective: To identify common principles and ideals

Goals of Participants: To spell out the initials of phrases of moral-based statements that the team shares in the fastest time

Overview: Prior to the game, the team brainstorms to come up with simple phrases that represent values and standards that each person wants to exemplify. The team is then timed by the facilitator to create an acronym and spell it out by lying on the ground and using their bodies to form the letters of the acronym. After the team accomplishes this once, then they perform the task again, attempting to decrease the amount of time that it takes.

Rules: The following are suggestions of value-based phrases and their acronyms:

- Choose the Right (CTR)
- Too Strong Together (TST)
- Together We Win (TWW)
- United We've Become (UWB)
- Together Brings Success (TBS)
- United We Stand (UWS)
- True to Each Other (TTEO)
- I Stand Not Alone (ISNA)
- We Can Do it Together (WCDIT)
- No One Gets Left Behind (NOGLB)

Preparation: The facilitator should provide each participant with a pad of paper and a pen for the brainstorming session. The facilitator also needs a stopwatch.

Location: Outdoors

Number of Participants: A team of 20

Age Range: 12 and older

Discussion Points: After the game, the facilitator should ask the following questions: How does identifying shared principles and ethics unify the team? What are other ways to illustrate these values using the acronym? The facilitator may wish to give the following suggestions: team name, cheer, song, T-shirts, superhero capes, or a flag.

Safety Precautions: As team members scramble to spell out the letters, caution should be taken to prevent colliding into other players.

Game #87: Paddleball and Mousetraps

Objective: To accomplish a task together by following order and rules

Goals of Participants: To set off mousetraps in a certain order using paddleballs

Overview: The team is timed to determine how fast they can set off mousetraps using paddleballs.

Rules: Prior to the game, each person is assigned a number from 1 to 5. The team members must take turns in the following order until all of the mousetraps are set off: 1, 2, 3, 4, 5; 5, 4, 3, 2, 1; 2, 3, 4, 5, 1. If a team member takes a turn out of order, a penalty of three minutes is added to the team's time. While waiting for his turn, each person should select a trap that he will set off and hold his paddleball as near to that trap as possible without touching it.

Preparation: The facilitator needs five paddleballs, 15 new mousetraps, and a stopwatch.

Location: Outdoors

Number of Participants: A team of five players

Age Range: Eight and older

Discussion Points: After the game, the facilitator should ask the following questions: What does "jumping the gun" mean, and how does it apply to this game? How is taking turns and following rules important in keeping peace among team members? What is greed? How can it destroy a team? What are ways that team members can avoid selfishness in a team setting?

Safety Precautions: Only the paddleballs should touch the mousetraps, and only new mousetraps should be used for this activity. The facilitator should be the only one setting the mousetraps.

Game #88: Blindfolded Zigzag Walk

Objective: To consider the mission and purpose of the team and how each person can make a difference toward the team's success

Goals of Participants: To walk blindfolded while carrying a cup of water

Overview: The facilitator lays a rope in a zigzag fashion on the floor. One at a time, each participant carries a cup filled with water while navigating along the rope with a blindfold on. The water in the cup symbolizes team spirit. Walking alone and preventing the water from spilling symbolizes the individual efforts that each person makes to ensure that he contributes to the affinity and camaraderie of the team. The zigzag of the rope symbolizes challenges or issues the team may face and reminds team members that they must stay close to issues until the issues are resolved.

Rules: No talking is allowed during this entire game and each person walks alone. As each participant finishes, he removes the blindfold and sits down to ponder his journey and think about how he can improve his contribution to the team.

Preparation: A long rope, a cup of water, and a blindfold are needed for this activity.

Location: Indoors or outdoors

Number of Participants: A team of five or more people

Age Range: Eight and older

Discussion Points: After the game, the facilitator should ask the following question: In what ways do you feel you can contribute to the success of the team's mission and purpose?

Safety Precautions: The facilitator should serve as a spotter for each participant to help him stay on course and keep his balance.

Game #89: Team Lunch

Objective: To function as one unit

Goals of Participants: To eat as a team with their hands tied together

Overview: Prior to lunch, the facilitator ties each team member's hands to two other team members' hands on either side of him. As a team, the group goes through the lunch line of a camp dining hall or a school cafeteria connected to each other. They must work together to put food on each other's plate.

Rules: As the group eats, each person must coordinate picking up his food and drinking from his cup with his hands tied to two other people's hands, one sitting on his right side and one on his left side. Not only does this activity require teamwork, but it also requires the patience and sacrifice of individual team members as each one waits his turn to feed himself. Giving up this basic need while serving others will bind a team together as they function as one unit.

Preparation: The facilitator needs string to tie both hands of each team member to other team members' hands.

Location: Indoor dining hall or cafeteria

Number of Participants: A team of five participants

Age Range: 12 and older

Discussion Points: After the game, the facilitator should ask the following questions: How does service to each other bind you together as a team to function as one unit? What are examples of other service opportunities that would unify you as a team?

Safety Precautions: The team should walk slowly to their table so no one stumbles or spills their food.

Game #90: Puzzle Personalities

Objective: To discover personal aspects of team members that will strengthen team relationships

Goals of Participants: To use their knowledge of each other to complete a puzzle

Overview: Each team member writes down something about himself on a puzzle piece, then all of the pieces are shuffled and each person takes a puzzle piece and takes a guess at who the piece belongs to. If his guess is correct, then he sets the piece on the table to be connected with other puzzle pieces as they are placed on the table. If the participant's guess is incorrect, then he waits for his turn again, and by the process of elimination, his chance to guess the correct person increases with each turn.

Rules: As more puzzle pieces appear on the table, team members are able to assemble the puzzle and unite the team's interests together. This event is not timed—in fact, the longer this activity takes, the more information about each participant is being acquired and understood.

Preparation: The facilitator needs a large, blank cardboard puzzle, markers, and a flat working surface to do the puzzle on, such as an indoor card table or an outdoor picnic table.

Location: Indoors or outdoors

Number of Participants: The same as the number of puzzle pieces (usually about 20)

Age Range: Eight and older

Discussion Points: After the game, the facilitator should ask the following questions: What are some things about other people that you discovered during the game? How could this information unite your team together to become stronger?

Safety Precautions: Only positive information—not self-defeating characteristics—should be listed, and no embarrassing situations should be revealed.

Game #91: Cookie Jars

Objective: To provide a fun opportunity to accomplish a task together

Goals of Participants: To gather up floating balls (cookies) in a swimming pool and put them inside floating hoops (cookie jars)

Overview: While the team is in the swimming pool, they gather four different colors of balls and put them in their color-coordinated hoops as quickly as possible (e.g., the red balls go inside the red hoop, the yellow balls go inside the yellow hoop, the blue balls go inside the blue hoop, and the green balls go inside the green hoop). The team plays two rounds of this game, attempting to improve its time with the second round.

Rules: In between the first and second rounds of the game, the team is encouraged to discuss ways to speed up the process of organizing the balls by identifying the strengths of each team member. For example, members that are good swimmers should go after the balls that are far away and bring them back. Members that can throw balls far should retrieve balls that have drifted out of the hoops and throw the balls to members who are good at catching. Team members with organizational skills should sort the balls and place them in corresponding hoops, and those team members with leadership skills should delegate these assignments with verbal guidance and support.

Preparation: The facilitator needs a bag of 100 plastic balls that are blue, red, yellow, and green and hoops in matching colors. A stopwatch is also needed.

Location: In an outdoor or indoor swimming pool

Number of Participants: A team of 15 players

Age Range: Eight and older

Discussion Points: After the game, the facilitator should ask the following questions: How did the team accomplish this task in unison? What was fun about this game? What was challenging about it? What are other team assignments that have a fun element yet are still challenging that you may face (for example, in sports)? Can these tasks also be accomplished in unison?

Safety Precautions: All participants should have strong swimming skills and this game should be played in a swimming pool where lifeguards are present. Everyone should watch for flying balls to avoid getting hit by them.

Game #92: Shrinking Circles

Objective: To develop problem solving skills collectively as a team, thus building stronger relationships

Goals of Participants: To fit in different rope circles as a team

Overview: The facilitator gives the team the challenge of putting their feet in four different sizes of rope circles. The first circle is a comfortable size for the team to stand in, but the second circle is smaller and requires much more effort for the group to stand in. The third circle is even smaller, and the team members have to really balance themselves in order to keep both feet in the circle. The fourth circle is impossible to fit everyone's feet into unless they think differently about possible solutions. The facilitator should allow the team plenty of time to brainstorm for solutions.

Rules: In order to complete the assignment, the team must reexamine the original challenge offered by the facilitator, which was to have all of the team members' *feet* in the circle at the same time. This task cannot be accomplished by the team members standing in the circle, rather they must lie on their backs with only their feet positioned in the fourth circle.

Preparation: The facilitator needs four rope circles of different sizes. The largest one should be three-and-a-half feet in diameter, and they should get progressively smaller, with the fourth one being one foot in diameter.

Location: Indoors or outdoors

Number of Participants: A team of four participants

Age Range: Eight and older

Discussion Points: After the game, the facilitator should ask the following questions: How did this game build affinity with the group? Did everyone have a chance to express their ideas and contribute solutions to the problem? Why is it important for everyone to contribute to the solution in order to strengthen team relationships?

Safety Precautions: Players should use caution when standing and balancing in the rope circles to ensure that they do not trip or stumble out of the circle. The facilitator should serve as a spotter as needed.

Game #93: Ping-Pong Balls and Bedsheet Funnel

Objective: To demonstrate how the roles of individual team members impact the team's success in accomplishing a difficult task

Goals of Participants: To get 10 Ping-Pong balls, one at a time, into a large cup in the shortest amount of time, using only a flat bedsheet

Overview: All team members need to hold onto the sheet and move the sheet around so that it functions as a funnel and deposits each ball into a receiving cup that is sitting on the ground.

Rules: Once a ball has been placed on the bedsheet, it can no longer be touched by anyone. The receiving cup cannot be moved from the ground or held in place by anyone on the team. If the cup tips over and the balls spill onto the ground, only the balls that actually touched the ground need to be passed through the bedsheet funnel again. Anytime a ball falls off the funnel, a team member should pick it up and put it back on the funnel to resume play. A leader of the game should be appointed by team members to give verbal guidance on how the sheet needs to move in order to direct the ball toward the receiving cup. Each team member should be alert and should be following the directions of the leader to know when to either lift or drop his section of the sheet to navigate the ball toward the cup.

Preparation: The facilitator needs a flat bedsheet, 10 Ping-Pong balls, a large cup, and a stopwatch.

Location: Indoors or outdoors

Number of Participants: A team of 10 players

Age Range: Six and older

Discussion Points: After the game, the facilitator should ask the following questions: How effective did each of you feel in moving the balls into the cup? How were the directions given by the leader helpful in accomplishing this task in the shortest amount of time? How did you feel about your specific role? Did your role contribute to building a stronger team relationship?

Safety Precautions: Players should use caution when playing this game to avoid stumbling over the dropped Ping-Pong balls.

Game #94: Team of Horses

Objective: To demonstrate the importance of individual effort in fulfilling a team assignment

Goals of Participants: To transport a bucket of balls as a team

Overview: The participants act as a team of horses to pull a rope connected to a tarp that functions as a stagecoach in order to carry a bucket of balls. Two people stand at the front of the tarp and two people stand at the back. The team must travel from a starting line to a finish line 25 feet away. Cones should be set up on the course to determine the starting line and finish line.

Rules: The bucket of balls carried on the tarp should be treated like "precious cargo," and if they get spilled, the team has to return to the starting line (i.e., the stagecoach station) and start the journey over again. This event is timed to see how quickly and efficiently the team can accomplish this task.

Preparation: The facilitator needs a small tarp, four pieces of six-foot rope, four cones, a small bucket of plastic balls, and a stopwatch.

Location: Outdoors

Number of Participants: Four players

Age Range: Eight and older

Discussion Points: After the game, the facilitator should ask the following questions: Did each team member pull his weight and assist the team in completing this assignment? How does the combined strength and stamina of four people help ease the burden of completing a difficult task? What impact does each person carrying his own load have on retaining positive relationships among team members?

Safety Precautions: The two people that are running in the front of the tarp must not run so fast that they end up dragging the two participants that are in the back of the tarp.

10

Reflection Games

Game #95: Warm Fuzzies

Objective: To reflect kindness and consideration

Goals of Participants: To give a tangible token of appreciation to fellow team members

Overview: This activity is done at the conclusion of a closing session. Each person is given five pom-poms and is told to give them to team members along with a compliment. Examples of these types of compliments are as follows: Thank you for your help today; I think you are a great leader; I appreciate your wisdom and insight in the things you said today; I have learned a lot from you; I have increased my trust in you today because of your strong leadership and example.

Rules: These expressions of gratitude do not need to be lengthy and elaborate, but they do need to be sincere.

Preparation: The facilitator needs five pom-poms for each team member.

Location: Indoors or outdoors

Number of Participants: A team of five or more participants

Age Range: Eight and older

Discussion Points: After the game, the facilitator should ask the following questions: How does gratitude unify a team? What other acts of kindness can be shown in a team setting?

Safety Precautions: These reflective moments, in which a participant expresses gratitude to another team member because of kindness that was originally shown to him during the team building events, should come naturally and be genuine. No team member should feel forced to offer this thank-you gift to others because such situations often result in resentment.

Game #96: Web of Appreciation

Objective: To unite and fortify the team through expressions of thoughtfulness

Goals of Participants: To create a session of thoughtful praise and recognition

Overview: The team stands in a circle and one person is given a ball of yarn with the instructions to hold onto the end piece but throw the ball gently to someone else while stating the leadership characteristic about that person that he admires the most.

Rules: Once the new person receives the ball of yarn, he identifies someone else in the circle and passes the ball of yarn and the expression of gratitude to them. This pattern continues until the string has connected the team together in a web of appreciation and praise. A physical bond pulls the team members together, but also an emotional bond is created through the verbal expressions of compassion.

Preparation: The facilitator will need a ball of yarn for this activity.

Location: Indoors or outdoors

Number of Participants: A team of 5 to 10 people

Age Range: Eight and older

Discussion Points: After the game, but while the participants are still holding onto the yarn in the web formation, the facilitator should illustrate that the team is connected to each other by tugging on one section of the web and pointing out that everyone on a team is impacted when communication—positive or negative—takes place in a team setting. However, the team is only fortified and strengthened when positive communication is exhibited.

Safety Precautions: The ball of yarn should be tossed gently underhand from one person to another, and all participants should be aware of where the ball is at all times to avoid being hit by it.

Game #97: Defining Leadership Characteristics

Objective: To exemplify leadership in a team setting

Goals of Participants: To identify and model leadership characteristics

Overview: Each team member is given a container of clay with the task of designing a symbol that represents a leadership quality that he admires most. Examples of these symbols include:

- A brain for wisdom
- A smile for a sense of humor
- A shield for devotion and faithfulness
- A heart for compassion
- A backbone for courage
- A book for knowledge
- A muscle for strength
- A flower for kindness
- A phone or computer for organizational and planning skills
- A hammer for a hard work

Rules: Each person has five minutes to design the symbol and then two minutes to describe it to team members.

Preparation: The facilitator will need a container of clay for each person and a stopwatch.

Location: Indoors or outdoors

Number of Participants: A team of 5 to 10 participants

Age Range: Eight and older

Discussion Points: After the game, the facilitator should ask the following question: How do you plan to exemplify these leadership characteristics in your personal life? The facilitator should point out other ways to learn about leadership traits such as reading books on great leaders, setting goals to become a leader, and practicing leadership traits with family and friends.

Safety Precautions: The facilitator should ensure that when each participant expresses himself, it is in a warm and receiving environment. Each person should be able to express what leadership means to him without negative feedback.

Game #98: Paint Can Processing

Objective: To create an environment where participants are comfortable asking questions

Goals of Participants: To write down questions anonymously about a teambuilding activity that the group just completed

Overview: The facilitator gives each participant three clean paint sticks to write any questions they may have about their teambuilding experience. Then, participants place their paint sticks in the paint can and the facilitator shuffles the sticks around and randomly pulls out one paint stick at a time, to answer each question. The reason for this activity is that some participants may still be processing some of the teambuilding elements or they could use a little more clarification in certain areas. This activity allows the facilitator to answer any questions that team members may have concerning leadership and teambuilding.

Rules: The questions can relate to the teambuilding activities or to the team in general.

Preparation: The facilitator needs a clean, unused paint can, markers, and three paint sticks per person.

Location: Indoors or outdoors

Number of Participants: A team of 5 to 10 people

Age Range: Eight and older

Discussion Points: Prior to this game, the facilitator should point out that a special feature of this activity is that each question is written on a paint stick that is identical to all of the other paint sticks and therefore each one is of equal value and does not stand out to embarrass a team member who may not have understood a certain leadership point. Each team member should be encouraged to write three thought-provoking questions that will help him better understand the leadership process he is currently experiencing by participating in teambuilding games with his team.

Safety Precautions: Only supplies that have not been used for painting should be acquired for this activity.

Game #99: Signal Mirror Course

Objective: To create reflection teaching moments after a teambuilding activity

Goals of Participants: To make signal mirrors as a way to learn the importance of reflection teaching moments in which the team processes the teaching elements of the teambuilding activities

Overview: Participants take two small, three-inch mirrors and use a piece of cotton ball with fingernail polish remover on it to wipe a pea-size hole in the center of the paint and metallic film on the back of both mirrors. Next, the two mirrors are lined up back to back and glued together to create a signal mirror that has two reflective sides with a hole in the center where light comes through. Each participant tries to find hidden license plates using his mirror. The reflective paint on the license plate will send a reflection back to the participant when the light from the mirror hits it.

Rules: The team works together to identify where all of the license plates are located.

Preparation: The facilitator needs two small, three-inch mirrors and a cotton ball for each participant, fingernail polish remover, superglue, and several license plates. Prior to the activity, the facilitator should hide the license plates in trees and bushes.

Location: Outdoors

Number of Participants: A team of five participants

Age Range: Eight and older

Discussion Points: After the game, the facilitator should ask the following questions: How is this reflection activity similar to a processing reflection activity where two-way communication allows team members to identify issues to strengthen the team? What can you learn from making signal mirrors that will help you in verbally communicating with team members? What does sending out a "signal" symbolize in developing team unity?

Safety Precautions: Participants should be warned to *never* look at the sun through the mirrors or direct the mirrors toward the sun.

Game #100: Fairy Tale Metaphor

Objective: To bring out the experiential elements of the leadership games played prior to this event

Goals of Participants: To draw comparisons between *The Wonderful Wizard of Oz* and a completed teambuilding session

Overview: At the end of the teambuilding session, a facilitator should refer to the story of *The Wonderful Wizard of Oz* by reading certain short segments from the book, reading a condensed version of the book, or just providing a brief overview of the story for those participants who are not familiar with the book or the movie. Then, he should ask the following questions:

- Which activity gave you courage like the Lion?
- Which activity made you think like the Scarecrow?
- What feelings of love and respect do you have toward your team members like the Tin Man?
- Were there any elements of an activity that frightened you like the flying monkeys?
- What obstacles did you overcome that seemed bigger than they really were like the Wizard of Oz's facade?

- What good things did you observe done by other people like the Good Witch of the North?
- What does the Wicked Witch of the West represent in your teambuilding experience?
- What were things the team could improve from your experience like Dorothy?
- What leadership paths lead to success like the yellow brick road?
- What fears can you overcome and dissolve through your service to other people, like the witch was dissolved when Dorothy put out the fire on the Scarecrow?
- What goals do the team have that will take you somewhere better like the ruby slippers?

Rules: Team members can draw out their own questions from their interpretation of the book as well.

Preparation: The facilitator needs a copy of the book *The Wonderful Wizard of Oz* or a condensed version of it such as a comic book or picture book.

Location: Indoors or outdoors

Number of Participants: A team of 5 to 10 participants

Age Range: Eight and older

Discussion Points: After the game, the facilitator can point out that teachable moments like this activity can occur in the most basic of situations and that team leaders should be aware and sensitive to these opportunities to teach and inspire.

Safety Precautions: Team members should feel comfortable sharing their ideas in a stress-free environment and not have to worry about what others may think of their answers.

Game #101: Brown Bag Questions

Objective: To provide team members the opportunity to ponder and process a leadership experience

Goals of Participants: To answer questions about a completed teambuilding experience based on random objects in a brown paper bag

Overview: Each team member is given a brown paper bag with a random item in it and when the participant pulls out the item, the facilitator asks that person one of the following corresponding questions:

- Glasses: What did you see during this experience that made you want to learn more?
- Whistle: What did you hear during the game that was a leadership principle?
- Key: What was the key to the leadership principle in this activity?
- Tape measure: How did this game measure success?
- Screwdriver: What were some twists and turns in this game?
- Chess piece: What part of the game made you think?
- First aid kit: How has this game aided the team?

- Dumbo's feather: What part of the game took the most courage and confidence?
- Rubber duck: What was something funny about this activity?
- Toy shark: What part of the activity seemed scary at first that you overcame your fear of in the end?
- Glue: How did the team become united?
- Sheriff's badge: Who was the leader of the game? Why?
- Domino: What actions of others impacted the whole team during the game? Was their impact good or bad?

Rules: The answers provided by team members should be brief so that each member has a turn to open his bag and respond to the contents inside.

Preparation: The facilitator needs paper bags and the items from the bulleted list, as well as a list of the corresponding questions to ask team members.

Location: Indoors or outdoors

Number of Participants: A team of 5 to 10 people

Age Range: Eight and older

Discussion Points: After the game, the facilitator should ask the following questions: How can these processing questions help the team remember the leadership principles that were learned? What are some goals that team members can immediately set to implement some of these leadership principles into the current team setting?

Safety Precautions: Each participant should be cautioned to slowly open his paper bag and carefully remove the contents when it is his turn.

About the Author

Since 1996, **Jared R. Knight** has been a member of the staff at Aspen Grove Family Camp, owned by Brigham Young University, where he currently serves as the manager of programs and human resources. In this position, he supervises programs and activities for more than 5,000 children during the summer camp and autumn weekend events. He also develops winter programming for 3,500 teenagers, providing faith-based youth conferences, where he organizes cross-country skiing and snowshoeing outings.

In preparing for this book, Knight used his experiences as a former Walt Disney World cast member, college intramural sports supervisor/referee, and certified ropes course facilitator to develop many of the ideas for games included in this text.

Knight is the former president of the American Camp Association, Southwest Section. He is the author of several well-received books, including *101 Creative Programs for Children*, *101 Age-Appropriate Camp Activities*, *101 Games and Activities to Strengthen Families*, and *101 Swimming Pool Games & Activities*. He is also the featured presenter of a 25-part DVD series on recreational programming. Knight has contributed more than 10 articles on program design to *Camp Business* magazine and is a popular speaker at many regional and national American Camp Association conferences.

Knight received a bachelor's in recreation management and youth leadership and a master's in public administration from Brigham Young University. He has also served as the director of development for United Way of Utah County and as a camp director for the Boy Scouts of America.

Knight and his wife, LaDonna, live in Utah with their three children, Rachel, Alex, and Emerson.